A Kiss
Beside the Monkey Bars

A Kiss
Beside the Monkey Bars
STORIES BY FOUR NEW WRITERS

Sultan Ameerali

Jennifer Lee

Kwai Li

Rosa Veltri

Life Rattle Press
Toronto, Canada

Life Rattle Press, Toronto, Canada

© 2004 by Life Rattle Press
and the authors

National Library of Canada Cataloguing in Publication

Main entry under the title:

A kiss beside the monkey bars: stories by four new writers / Sultan Ameerali ... [et al.].

(Life rattle new writers series 1200-5266-17)
ISBN 978-1-927023-83-1

1. Short stories, Canadian (English) 2. Canadian fiction (English)--21st century. I. Ameerali, Sultan, 1977- II. Series.

PS8321.K49 2004   C813'.010806   C2004-900896-X

Printed and bound in Canada

Cover Design by Laurie Kallis
Cover Art by Laurie Kallis
Typesetting by Kwai Li and Laurie Kallis

Dedicated to

The Erindale Writers Group

Contents

Acknowledgments 1

Introduction 3

Sultan Ameerali   BK Variety: A Story in Two Parts 9

SkyDome: Death of a Thousand Cuts . . 17

Condom Mania. 21

My Valentine's Day Rant 27

Crap Lobby. 31

One Night in a Basement Apartment. . . 49

Tattoo—Blow Job Story 63

Jennifer Lee   The Red-Brick Path. 77

Easter Lilies. 85

Derrick 97

Chinese Christmas 103

Beijing Heat. 109

Copenhagen Mermaid. 115

Rosa Veltri

Maria Florentina 133

Cotton Undershirt 153

Tipper's Fruit Market 155

The Bakery 165

Christmas Party 177

Half a Case of Oranges 185

A Heater and a Fan 191

A Ballerina and a Nurse 207

Kwai Li

Farewell, Calcutta 217

A Fish Who Invited Itself to Dinner. . . 231

The East Is Red 235

Police Raid on Moonshine Pond 247

Woody and Mei Ling 255

The Godfather of Chinatown 267

Long Live Mao Tse Tung 281

Acknowledgments

In 1999, Guy Allen approached the four writers in this collection about a book of short stories. He said, "People should read these stories. People should hear these voices." Guy Allen's encouragement and vision propelled this project to its completion.

Many thanks to Guy Allen, Arnie Achtman, Laurie Kallis, Vaia Barkas, Martha Ayim and the members of the Erindale Writers Group, for suggestions and editing.

Many thanks to New Writers' Initiative who underwrote the costs of publication.

Most of these stories first appeared as broadcasts on *Life Rattle*, a radio program dedicated to new writing, CKLN, 88.1 FM, Sunday evenings from 9:00 - 9:30.

Introduction

The New Writers' Initiative has supported the project with money and expertise. The four writers in this book advance the New Writers Initiative mission: to see into print work rooted in Toronto communities that we read too little about in published literature.

We who love Toronto love that we see so much of the world in our city. We can never see enough of the cultural depth people like the writers of *Monkey Bars* bring to Canada. These writers lead Canadian lives rooted in China, India, Sri Lanka, Italy.

Sharp, supportive editing grounded *Monkey Bars*. Writers supported writers. Their stories prod us to see things behind the faces we pass on our streets.

New Writers' Initiative
July 2004

Sultan Ameerali

SULTAN AMEERALI, born to Sri Lankan immigrants, in Toronto in 1977, the third of four boys, financed his education with "bottom-feeder" jobs. He earned his undergraduate degree from the University of Toronto and postgraduate diploma in journalism from Centennial College. Ameerali currently lives in Toronto and works as editor for an all-news radio station.

↙ Intense Story

BK Variety: A Story in Two Parts

Part 1: Garbage Man Selling du Mauriers

On winter mornings, BK Variety not only warmed like an oven but also shone like a beacon in darkness. Salim came in from the frigid darkness outside and walked behind the counter.

"You're early," I said to him. "I don't finish until six."

"I need the hours. I know you like to take off early. I thought I could pick up an extra hour."

"Forget it."

"Why the hell not?"

"Man, use your head. It's five in the morning! Where the fuck am I supposed to go? The subway doesn't open until five-thirty. I may as well work the extra thirty minutes."

"I came all this way for nothing? Have to hang around with you for an hour?"

"What, this is my fault!? Who told you to come in? Besides—hold on a second."

A man came up to the counter.

"Du Maurier large King, please."

I rang him up. "Four dollars."

"No no man," he said. "I'm down."

9

"Oh, sorry."

I reached under the counter and got him another pack of du Maurier King and took back the first one I gave him. The new pack lacked a duty stamp.

"Three dollars."

"Thanks, man," he said as he picked up his cigarettes and left.

I took the three loonies and put them in the little box under the counter.

"Man, I don't know why you go along with that shit. Anybody asks me, I just tell'em we're out, which is true half the time anyway."

"What do I care?"

"If you get bit, I think there's a fine or something. You might go to jail."

"So what, let the fat fuck pay it. He owns the place."

"No man, not him. You," Salim said, pointing at me. "Why do think he never sells them himself? How many times you wanna get bit for him? Didn't you already get a ticket for selling to a 'minor'?" Salim mimed the quotation marks with his fingers.

I nodded. A kid no more than five years old had come in to buy cigarettes. When I told him he was too young, he left. Half an hour later, he came back with a letter from his mother. I sold him a pack because the letter amused me. As we completed the purchase, two cops came in for a Lotto 6/49.

"That's true," I said. "That last ticket ate half my cheque. Anyway, why are you here?"

"I need hours. I wanna take my woman someplace good for Valentine's Day."

"Hold on a sec," I said.

An old man came up to the counter with a newspaper.

"Du Maurier please."

BK Variety: A Story in Two Parts

"Four dollars and sixty cents."

"Why four dollars and sixty cents?"

"Four dollars for the cigarettes and sixty cents for the newspaper."

"But newspapers are only fifty cents from the box."

"Ten cents for service."

"Why would I pay ten cents for service when I can get a paper from the box for—"

"Is this the fucking box!? You wanna buy from the box, buy from the fucking box! You wanna buy from me, it's sixty fucking cents!"

He paid the four sixty and left.

"Every day with this guy...anyway, what? You need cash for your woman?"

"Yeah man."

"You're a sucker. Coming in early hoping to get an extra hour just so you can spend it on a woman. Pathetic."

"I don't see *you* with a woman."

"You don't get it, do you? Guys like you and me, we're just the garbage men. We drive around in—you still driving that Reliant?"

"Yeah man. K-cars rule."

"We come around in our K-cars, and we pick up whatever fresh piece of garbage was just dumped on the curb by someone who was either smarter and/or better looking. So why break the bank?"

We stood there in awkward silence listening to the hum of the freezer when a regular-looking guy walked into the store.

"Pack of du Maurier Filters," Mr. Regular said as he pulled out exact change.

As I rang him up, Salim said, "You know, I respect you man. Working the overnight and shit. I mean, hell if you're not working the overnight, he just closes up the store. No one else will work it but...." His voice trailed off. "I mean, that garbage man stuff, that's just warped."

"What! You think I'm wrong? I'm just telling you what you should already know. You mean to tell me if that chick who buys the Rothmans Ultra Lites asked you out you would say, 'I'm already seeing somebody right now. But thanks anyway'?"

Salim scrunched his face and thought.

"Exactly! Why do you think we tell the fat fuck to buy Ultra Lites? Ultra Lites are like smoking the clippings from your lawn mower. Nobody smokes them except her. Get smart, man. Maybe you know this, maybe you don't, but size matters."

"Look, I don't know about you but...."

"Not that, you idiot. You and me, we're about the same height five-foot-four, five-foot-five, about a 110 pounds. The average male is five-foot-eight. Women will let a lot of shit go. You may not have a job, a car, any prospects for the future—but they'll let that go. If you're even one inch under five foot eight, forget about it."

"So what am I supposed to do? I've done *did* all the growing I'm going to do."

"That's what I'm saying! You're a fucking garbage man. Blame romance novels. Blame Brad Pitt. Blame whoever the fuck you want. But just admit it and don't waste your money."

"Can I get a du Maurier Light King?" a lady said as she came to the counter.

As I rang her up, I finished my sermon. "Nothing personal. I'm just trying to save you some cash, that's all. Look, it's like five-twenty, and you probably saved me a fine. I'll punch out at five. You take this hour."

"Nah. For some reason I don't feel like it anymore."

BK Variety: A Story in Two Parts

We said nothing and looked at the overstuffed shelves and the cramped aisles, at the security camera behind us, at the mirror in the far corner reflecting the back aisle and the slush on the floor.

"Garbage men, huh?" Salim said.

"Garbage men. Don't feel bad about it. Even if you weren't a garbage man, you still wouldn't get any play. If you were a woman, would you go out with someone who worked here?"

Part 2: The Night Shift at BK Variety

I summon all my will power to pull my head off the counter and look around. It's still dark outside, but the wind has kicked up a bit since I checked last. I look at my watch—4:36 a.m.—almost ninety minutes have gone by since I last looked at my watch. I look at the store and everything is exactly the same.

Coppery stains still run down the side of the coffee machine by the door. Used filters still stuff a coffee pot beside the machine. And the coffee pot under the machine still sits half-full of ice-cold, caffeine-infested sludge. I cannot bring myself to clean the coffee machine. It smells bad, like rancid barbecue. The magazine rack, across the store from the coffee machine, still holds the same array of month-old car magazines, erotica and pornography. I run down my mental checklist and find everything exactly the same. All the same crap and garbage that BK Variety always sells is in the same place. It's one of those nights where nobody comes in and I feel every agonizing minute go by.

I pull a pack of Player's Lights off the precious cigarette shelf behind me. In west Scarborough, cigarettes are the gateway to a magic land and I am the gatekeeper. After ripping through cellophane, I light one, take a drag, hold the smoke in my lungs and slowly open my mouth. My head feels five pounds lighter. I look down at my *Toronto Star*, prepared now to attack the Jumble puzzle once again.

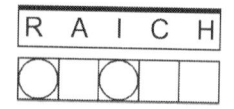

R	A	I	C	H
◯	◯			

R_A_I_C_H. I repeat the letters to myself for the hundredth or the two hundredth or maybe the three hundredth time. "God dammit!" I yell at the empty store. I'm this close to figuring it out.

I get up off the stool and feel a thousand needles in my legs as my knees buckle. I grab the cash register and free a thick plume of smoke from my lungs.

"Fucking legs are asleep! I need to stretch!" I yell, coughing up the last few words. Yelling with nobody in the store serves two purposes. One, it relieves stress, and two, anybody outside the store thinking of coming in the store, will probably think again.

I look down at the stool. The padding is compressed. Yellow foam oozes from a tear in the corner of the black vinyl seat.

"Fucking fat pantloads on the day shift are killing the stool! I can't sit on this anymore! I'm getting chairass! Fucking chairass! CHAIRASS!" I scream.

I sit back down. So much for stretching.

R-A-I-C-H. R-A-I-C—fucking—*H!*

As I repeat my chant, the door opens and a tall spindly kid strides towards the counter with his arms limp at his sides—a version of the pimp roll. His yellow construction boots clunk as he pimp rolls his way towards me.

Clunk. Clunk. Clunk.

Then I notice the panty hose on his face.

BK Variety: A Story in Two Parts

The kid puts his hand in his pocket.

Clunk. Clunk.

I look under the counter. The baseball bat and the crowbar that are supposed to be there, aren't.

Clunk.

The kid stops and pulls a small revolver from his bulky winter jacket.

I'm a dead man.

He extends his arm, holds the gun sideways and fires—above me and to the left. He shoots at the security camera in the corner.

Pop! Pop! Pop! Pop! Dust from the cracked and dirty drywall mingles with the dust from behind the cracked and dirty drywall creating a giant dirt cloud around the camera. We both wait for the dust to clear as flecks of the wall flutter to the floor. Five seconds pass. Then ten seconds. I realize my cigarette is still in my mouth. I want to take a drag, but can't breathe.

Finally the dust clears and the red light under the lens of the security camera shines through the haze. I turn and look at the kid. Our eyes lock for a split second in joint disbelief.

"*Sheeit!*" he says as he turns and clunks out of the store.

I sit for a while and stare at the sour cream and onion chips across from me. My Player's Light burns down to the filter and the ash on the end of the cigarette comes close to breaking off. Then it hits me.

R-A-I-C-H. C-H-A-I-R. Chair! Chair! It's chair. I move onto the last Jumble. Let the day shift call the cops.

    S U S C S I D
    □ ○ □ ○ □ □ □

S-U-S-C-S-I-D. S-U-S-C-S-I-D. I'm close. I'm close. I can feel it.

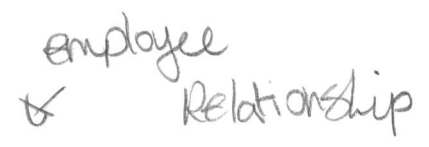

SkyDome: Death of a Thousand Cuts

Bleat! Bleat! Bleat! Bleat! Bleat! The alarm screams. It pierces my deep sleep. In the darkness the red display glows 4:30. I let the alarm bleat long enough to wake me, but not long enough to wake Marla. I resist the temptation to hit the snooze. *Bleat! Bleat! Bleat! Ble———.* I hit the off switch. I turn to face Marla and all I see is the wall. My heart sinks as I remember that Marla is asleep in Mississauga and I'm awake in Scarborough.

I plod to the washroom. In seconds my eyes adjust to the light. I brush my teeth. I wash and shave my face. I hate shaving. Without facial hair I look fifteen, but SkyDome has a no-facial-hair policy. I smile as I think of my don't-wash-my-hands policy. I get dressed and stick two granola bars and a carton of Beckers 2% milk in my pockets.

By five-thirty, I wait at the corner of Morningside and Sheppard for the 116 bus. Despite sixteen hours of sunlight, I go to work when it's pitch black outside. It depresses me that I recognize the *Con Air* advertisement and the 7426 bus number. It depresses me that I nod to the bus driver. It depresses me that I recognize every face on the bus, the overweight lady with the Rasta hat, the grubby factory worker and the spaced-out deadhead, and they recognize me. I know them. Oh God, I know them. It depresses me that I know the bus will pull into Kennedy Station in exactly twenty-five minutes.

Exactly twenty-five minutes later, *Con Air* bus 7426 pulls into Kennedy Station.

A subway to Yonge. A subway to Union. I feel alive as I walk up the stairs to the main level of Union Station. Sunlight shines on the clean marble floor through the glass ceiling of the SkyWalk. The click of my shoes echoes through the building. I look up at the clock—6:35. I feel dead again. I start work in twenty-five minutes.

I enter Gate 3 and nod to the skinny kid behind the counter. His uniform is too big and he watches the clock. He probably finishes at seven o'clock, the graveyard shift. I swipe my ID card and head onto the elevator. Ding! The doors part. Almost two and a half hours and I've finally arrived.

I walk through the cafeteria into the locker room, acknowledging no one. I never say hello or good morning. Since I started working at the SkyDome there has never been a good morning.

I finish changing into my uniform by putting on my paper hat. It's time to go to work.

I walk past Peter and sign in: 7:05. Peter, the assistant chef, is British, tall, muscular and dedicated to this job—my opposite.

If it were up to Peter, I would be unemployed.

"In my office *now!*" Peter says, laying on the British accent extra limey.

Limey motherfucker! I just signed in. What the fuck could I have done?

I follow him into the office. He throws a veggie platter onto the table. The tray smacks on the desk. Coloured stickers ornament Saran Wrap covered platter. The blue Monday tag, the red Tuesday tag and the green Wednesday tag are plastered over each other.

SkyDome: Death of a Thousand Cuts

"I've been getting complaints. 'The trays smell. The vegetables are rotten.' But I think, no, that couldn't be. Sultan wouldn't do that. So I check the freezer and I'm repulsed by ten of these!" Peter violently jabs his finger at the rancid tray on his desk.

He continues his tirade and I stare at the tray. It's everything I can do not to laugh—a second Monday tag peeks out from under a brown Sunday tag. Just how old is this thing?

"If you were incompetent that would be one thing, but this is just sheer laziness! You couldn't even be bothered to peel off the old tags 'fore you put on the new ones!" he screams.

I can sense the number of people within earshot increasing exponentially.

Limey fuck! Fire me! Fire me!

Peter and I lock in a battle of wills. I won't quit, because if Peter fires me, I get a week of severance pay. Peter won't fire me because he over budgeted on overtime.

"...You're being a dick. Your dicketry—"

Dick! Dicketry! I'm not taking this limey bullshit from some punk. A limey punk! This ain't Manchester! I'm from Scarborough! I'm hardcore! It's time to get ethnic on his limey ass. I can see rage in his eyes. It's time to push him over the edge.

"Man, just chill out *bra*."

Peter's eyes go blank.

"Bra? Did you just call me a bra?"

Laughter erupts outside the office.

Peter's face flushes.

"I said *bra*', like brother. Not bra as in...well bra."

Cooks and dishwashers stream into the office and do their best British "bra" impersonation. Peter grins as he wades through the

19

crowd of workers who laugh and slap his back. I leave fuming. I had him so close to firing me and now we're *bras*.

I go into the freezer and sit down on some bread racks. I can see the long breath I let out. I pull out my two granola bars, my carton of Beckers 2% milk, and I have my breakfast. I think about calling Marla and remember she's probably still asleep. It's only 7:15 in the morning…my day is only beginning.

Home $ werk

Condom Mania

I finished brushing my teeth and turned off the bathroom light. I stretched my arms wide and yawned long and loud as I walked into the bedroom. I hadn't slept in over twenty-four hours. The long day at work, then school, left me ready to collapse. I stopped in the doorway.

Marla lay on the near side of the double bed, leaning back against the metal headboard, comforter pulled up to her knees, reading a blue textbook called *Out from Underdevelopment Revisited*. She looked beautiful as always. The soft light from the bedside lamp illuminated the subtle curves of her hips and her long, curly brown hair. She wore one of my dress shirts to bed, buttoned up only halfway. From my angle I could see most of her right breast.

Marla was my woman—in fact, we were engaged. One night a few months ago, we split two thirty-ounce bottles of Absolut vodka and after having wild drunken sex on the floor I said to her, "We should get married someday," and she said, "Okay."

To my horror, when we sobered up the next day she not only held me to that, but she told every person she encountered afterwards that she was engaged.

I stood in the doorway and watched her read her book.

After four pages of *Out from Underdevelopment Revisited*, she looked up at me, smiled and said, "Are you coming to bed or aren't you?"

I decided to take advantage of the only redeeming quality of the cohabitating-engaged-to-be-married-at-some-abstract-point-in-the-future-college-students-in-love relationship: the ability to have sex any time I want. I got a running start and leaped over Marla into bed.

She laughed as she dropped her book on the floor and put her arms around me. I kissed my "fiancée" hard on the lips as I undid the buttons of her shirt. I was about to get laid. I had the world by the ass. Then Marla opened her mouth.

"Wait," she said softly as she broke off the kiss.

"Wait? For what?"

"Where's your condom?"

"I don't have a condom," I said as I brushed her wild hair out of her face. "Now let's continue where we left off, shall we?" She pulled her head away as I tried to kiss her.

"Wait. What do you mean you don't have a condom?"

I started to get annoyed but I tried to reason with her. "One time is not going to matter. Now can we get on with this?"

"Yes. One time is going to matter."

"Will you stop worrying? You're on the pill. One time isn't the end of the world. Do you know how small the odds are on this? Do you understand the underlying science? Trust me—I'm a physics major."

"What are you talking about? I'm not on the pill!"

"You're not. Really? I didn't know that." I jerked back from her as she exploded into a fury of flailing arms.

"No, I'm not on the pill! We've been fucking each other almost three years and you don't know if I'm on the pill or not?" She yelled as she did up the buttons on her shirt all the way to the collar.

"Of course not. Why would I? I just sort of assumed that you were."

"You're a pig!"

I took a deep breath, rubbed my temples and leaned back against the headboard. "Why...aren't you on the pill?"

"I don't take the pill. I'm a good girl."

"What the fuck does that mean!? In that case, I can't clean the bathroom because...well just because."

"You wouldn't understand," she answered, "and you better clean that bathroom, it's disgusting."

"Look, I don't know what kind of scam you're trying to pull. You're not a good girl. You're an idiot. You give me grief, you drink all my liquor and now I find out you don't take the pill. What's the real reason?"

"When I was sixteen Papa came into my room one day and begged me never to use the pill. He just barges in and he's like: 'You're a good girl. You've always been a good girl. Now swear to God you'll never use it! Swear!' What can I do? I swore to God. I'm stuck. I just can't believe you didn't realize."

"Why would I want to know something like that? I just assumed, I mean, it doesn't make any sense for you not to take it," I said.

"So what are you saying? That it's my responsibility to use protection?"

"No, I'm saying that it would make sense to have a safety net. Hell, it would have been nice if you had said something. I've been using these second rate free condoms they give out at Hart House."

"What!" she screamed. "Are you crazy!? What are you using free condoms for!? You get what you pay for. Are you trying to start a family or something?"

"You better back off woman!" I said, as I leaned toward her and put my finger in her face.

Just as quickly, she swatted it away.

"I'm paying for rent, tuition—food! My daddy isn't paying the freight for me. I'm on a tight budget here. I cut corners wherever I can."

We lay on the bed, silent and still, without looking at each other in the dimly lit room. After several minutes, Marla spoke.

"Are there any condoms in the house anyway?"

"In the wardrobe, in a shopping bag."

"Why don't you go get one and we'll put this whole thing behind us," she said. A smile snuck across her face. "How about that?"

"Nah, I don't think so." I rolled over and turned off the lamp.

"What do you mean, 'I don't think so'?" she shot back from the dark.

I turned on the lamp and rolled back. "You want to depend on a condom from the University of Toronto? I'm supposed to trust the U of T to prevent pregnancy? I don't even trust U of T to provide quality education and I pay them four grand a year for that. I got the condoms for free, so what are they worth? Besides, I don't feel like it anymore."

"You don't feel like it anymore?" The words came out of her throat tight and slow.

"Yeah, it was more of a spur of the moment type of thing, you know. The end of a long day spent solving math problems with ugly, *ugly*, men. You were lying in bed reading and you looked beautiful—not that you don't look beautiful now—and well...it was the moment, you know, but now the moment has passed. You know what I'm saying?"

"No," she said, shaking her head. "I don't have any fucking clue what the hell you're saying. Now go over there and get one of those damn things out of the bag and come back here."

This was too good of an opportunity to pass up.

"Boy. I didn't realize that you wanted it so bad. But if you need it that bad then I'll go and—"

"Oh no you don't, you son-of-a-bitch," she interrupted. "Don't you dare try to hang this on me! You're just too lazy to roll out of bed and go get a condom—aren't you? That's why you're not interested anymore—isn't it? My God, you've got to be the laziest man I've ever seen! Are you gay? What kind of heterosexual man turns down sex? You're a hump!"

"I'm not a hump."

"You're a hump! A fag hump at that!"

"Look, woman! I'm not a hump. I'm sure as hell not gay! I'm tired. I worked an overnight shift and went straight to school. My body is tired." I paused for effect. "My brain is tired." I pointed at the wardrobe. "If you want to have sex so bad, you go over there and get the condom your damn self, otherwise I'm going to sleep."

I waited and she did nothing. As I reached over to turn off the lamp she muttered, "Gee, you are so fucking lazy." I froze in mid-reach and turned back to face her.

"I'm lazy?! You're so lazy you won't even pop one lousy pill a night. How's that for lazy! And don't give me that garbage about your dad. You know as well as I do, no matter how angry your crazy cracker of a father would get that you're using the pill, that 'Papa' would be colossally more pissed off if you brought him a grandson with wavy black hair and a tan. Ipso facto that makes you," I leaned over and tapped her on the cheek, "the queen of laziness. You know, I'm surprised I have to admit...."

"Surprised?" She asked. "Why?"

"Because for most chicks, it's like a mark of honour to be on the pill."

"A mark of honour?" She spat out the words.

"Yeah. You know, like they brag about it. They go up to their friends and they say, 'Guess what Marla? I'm on the pill.' And they wave around the little circular dispenser and they brag about how they're taking the pink one today but that's not really a pill, it's just sugar and stuff like that. It's like a badge that says you're having sex or think you're going to have sex in the near future."

Marla's face turned a bright scarlet and she buried her head in my chest as she laughed. When she finally stopped, she clamped her hands on my shoulders, brought her face close to mine and looked into my eyes. "I can't believe you just said that. Before we went out you didn't deal with women for a long time, did you?"

"Whatever. Can I please go to sleep now?"

She cracked up again. "Yeah, you can go to sleep," she said between bouts of laughter. "Maybe you should sleep by yourself for a while. It'll cure you of whatever possessed you to say something like that. You want some tea?" She climbed out of bed and walked into the kitchen.

"Whatever," I yelled after her. "You think you can threaten me by withholding sex?"

"Yeah," she yelled back.

"I'm short and I major in physics. I'm a garbage man! I'm used to not having sex."

I turned out the light and fell asleep.

My Valentine's Day Rant

"So what do you want to do?" I ask Marla as I get in the car. I already know the answer. Today is February 14th. The answer is always the same on February 14th.

"Let's see a movie."

"A movie. Why don't we—"

"Why do you even bother asking me?" she interrupts. "If you have something you want to do, then just say—"

"Fine!" I sigh. "We'll see a movie."

Marla peels out of the driveway and speeds through a red light at Glen Erin Drive.

I stare out the window at fields of dead grass.

A movie on Valentine's Day! How original. God forbid we go to a restaurant and have dinner like classy people. Of course, today is Friday so movies cost full price. I hate Valentine's Day. They should rename it Something-for-Nothing day. Every year, the same drill—I pay through the nose. Between the $19.50 for the crappy bear (For a bear that small? I hope it was stuffed with gold) and $18.00 for the movie tickets, Valentine's Day has already cost me $37.50.

Marla slows for the yellow at Eglinton and I stare at a busty young lady, wearing a red tube top, crossing the street. I already know what Marla will give me for Valentine's Day. Before she started the car she said she had "something special planned" for later tonight. Unless Marla got a sense of originality when I wasn't looking, "something special" means sex. The problem is we have sex two times a week anyway, so I don't see how she can call it "something special." Usually "something special" sex consists of usual sex with a scented candle or incense burning on top of the wardrobe. Really, would it kill her to just get me a bottle of Jim Beam?

The final insult? When I gave her the crappy bear, I think I could have got a better reaction if I gave her a tube of Bengay. Maybe I should have left the price tag on.

"So what do you want to see?" Marla says to me with that hint of malice in her voice that tells me she knows exactly what she wants to see and that she saw me stare at Miss Red Tube Top. I know better than to answer her straight. Play it cool. That's the way to go. Marla floors the gas on the green and my head wrenches back.

"I don't have anything particular in mind," I say. "Yourself?" Please say James Bond, I think to myself. I want to see the new James Bond movie, but more importantly I want to see Teri Hatcher in the new James Bond movie.

"How about that new Van Damme movie?" Marla says.

Van Damme!? What kind of space cadet am I dealing with? I'm not paying eighteen bucks so you can ogle some guy in a sweaty T-shirt. When Jean Claude Van Damme spends $37.50 on her, then she can watch his crappy movie. The James Bond movie plays for the last time today. I'm watching the James Bond movie. I'm getting something out of my $37.50.

"What about that new James Bond movie? What's it called, *Tomorrow Never Dies*?" I say. "I'm not sure, but I think it's still playing at the Coliseum."

My Valentine's Day Rant

"Fine, no problem. But I think it's kind of long. Let's get something to eat first."

Food! $37.50 and it doesn't even cover food. If we stop for food we'll miss James Bond. Buy movie food and today's tab will be over sixty bucks. This hurts either way.

"We'll get something at the theatre," I mumble, but I think she hears me.

"You're in a good mood today," she says. "I've never seen you buy movie food. You're always complaining about being gouged." Marla flashes her teeth and puts her hand on my shoulder.

Good mood? I'm dying here and she thinks I'm in a good mood. Get your hand off of me, woman! Do I really want to be here? I'm out sixty bucks. For sixty dollars, I could hire a cheap hooker. For sixty dollars, I could have thirty minutes of phone sex. Why would I spend sixty dollars on this woman? I make twelve dollars an hour. That's five hours of pay gone. I work as a night watchman. I could get shot. I risked my life for this sixty and now I'm spending it on her? I risked my life for a crappy bear, movie tickets and a gallon of synthetic butter. An incense candle costs sixty-five cents. By my rough estimate, Marla owes me $59.35 or she has to have "something special" sex with me about ninety times later tonight.

I look away from the other cars toward the sky as we turn onto Burnhamthorpe. Marla waits for me to tell her why I am in a good mood.

"Today is a special day," I say in the most sincere voice I can muster.

I have no spine. I have no spine at all.

I turn on the radio. My brother says turning on the radio fills a conversation vacuum. He's right. We go the rest of the way without saying anything. If only I could bring the radio with me for the rest of the night.

I could probably get a really good radio for sixty dollars.

Crap Lobby

11:30 p.m.

I waited for a lull in the traffic along Yonge Street before I ran for the double set of glass doors of the tall, aqua-tinted and mirror-skinned office building across the street. In the yellow flourescent light that shone from the concrete awning, I saw the cold December rain that pounded into my jacket. My cold, stiff fingers, covered with thin, black, worn leather gloves, fumbled with the plastic security card and ran the card through once, twice, three times before the door beeped and opened.

"Hey man," I said to Esan as I walked into the spacious marble lobby past the koi pond.

As usual, I arrived five minutes late.

"How's it going little bro'?" he replied. His face buried behind a *Playboy* with Carmen Electra on the cover. He pulled his feet down off the counter. "Hey, did you bring it?" he asked. "Please tell me you brought it."

"Don't worry. I brought it." I peeled off my wet jacket and scarf.

"Did you bring any coffee? I can't stay awake."

"No man, it's really coming down outside. I'll cover you here if you want to go get some."

Esan looked outside at the downpour, admired voluptuous curves as he flipped through a couple of pages of his *Playboy*, looked outside again, then said, "Don't worry about it. I'll be just fine. Enough about coffee though, let's see what you got."

I hung my jacket on the back of a cushioned aquamarine seat and pulled my clip-on tie from the pocket.

"Let me see. Let me see." He sounded more like a little child than a portly Russian security guard with ring-around-the-collar.

"Hold on!" I said as I clipped on my tie and smoothed out the wrinkles.

"Let. Me. See. It." Esan whined.

"Alright you fat bastard! Here it is."

I pulled out a gold box with a green ribbon. The ribbon had gold frills and tied a pink envelope to the box. Inside the envelope was a birthday card. The small box had the words *Godiva Chocolatiers* engraved on it in large letters. I handed Esan the box.

"This looks expensive," Esan said. He rotated the box in his hand.

"I checked. It's sixteen dollars at the Bay," I said as I watched the monitor. It showed a guy in the elevator with a bald spot you could only have seen if you stood directly over him. I watched the guy scratch his ass. Maybe he thought nobody could see him.

Esan took off the ribbon. "Kind of small." He set aside the card and lifted the lid. "How many chocolates are in here?"

"Four."

"Four! Sixteen dollars for four chocolates!" Esan pulled away the cotton and looked at the chocolates. "Hey, these are all—"

"Yes," I interrupted him, "yes, they are."

The chocolates were all shaped like hearts.

"Do you mind?" Esan picked up one of the chocolates.

Crap Lobby

"Nah. Go ahead. Those things have caused me enough problems."

Ding! The elevator bell rang, its doors split apart and Mr. Ass Scratcher walked out into the lobby.

Esan chewed quickly as he swept the box and the magazine into an open drawer.

I picked up the flashlight on the counter and walked to the window where a bum slumped over the grate outside.

Even though he crouched against the glass the bum seemed tall. Was he stocky? Was he thin? I couldn't tell. A stained grey trench coat with loops for a belt but no belt wrapped around his body. Filth crusted his face and hands and his beard came down to the collar of his shirt. He wore a derby pulled down tight on his head. The derby had a rip in the brim and what looked like a ketchup stain.

I tapped the glass and shone the light in his face. I waved the flashlight in the standard move-it-along gesture.

"Fucking Paki!" he screamed in a hoarse, grating voice. "Can't you just leave me in peace? It is fucking freezing."

I wish I could, I thought. But it's either you or me.

Mr. Ass Scratcher walked slowly with his nose tipped into the air, eye-fucking us all the way to the exit. He tried his best to look majestic in a black trench coat he probably got on sale from Sears. It didn't work.

"Fucking Ass Scratcher! Vot da fok his problem," Esan said. When he got upset Esan's thick Russian accent got even thicker.

"Do you think he knows?" I said to Esan.

"Knows? Please! The only 'knows' that ass-scratching cock smoker knows anything about is that big honker on the end of his mother-fucking face."

Esan and I lounged in the Ass Scratcher's office every opportunity we got. The Ass Scratcher was, in actuality, Mr. Marois. We didn't know what he did. But we knew Mr. Marois had the biggest office on the fifteenth floor. The office had plush green carpeting, a home stereo, a plastic palm tree and a right-angled silver velvet couch that fit snugly into the corner of his office. Most importantly, Mr. Marois' office had a Sony Trinitron fifty-inch projection television. Esan and I took turns watching TV in the lap of ass-scratching luxury.

"Still, we shouldn't have took those doughnuts up there last week," I said. "You spilled powder everywhere. And you threw the box in his garbage can, you fucking idiot!"

"So?"

"So I think he's going to remember if he ate a box of fucking Dunkin' Donuts."

"Maybe. Okay, new rule," Esan said, stifling a yawn. "No food in the Ass Scratcher's office. So anyway, let's get back to this box of yours. What happened?" Esan barely got the words out as he pulled the gold box out of the drawer and gorged on another two chocolates.

"Some chick in my electromagnetic class gave that to me yesterday for my birthday."

"I thought your birthday was in November. Why did I buy you a beer in November if your birthday is in December?"

"It is in November. I wanted to blow off a lab assignment so I told her my license was expiring in a couple of days. Apparently your license expires on your birthday. I should think my lies through better."

"Maybe she's just being friendly. It doesn't mean anything."

"Read the card, man," I said.

Crap Lobby

Esan pulled the card out of the pink envelope and scanned it, mumbling the key words out loud.

"Ziggy says...Happy Birthday...Best wishes...Special Day...Love. Love? You're in big trouble, man."

"I already know that. What I need from you is what I should do about it?"

"Do about it? This is good, man, take this chippie for a ride." He smiled, rolled up his *Playboy* and whacked me on the back.

"I don't think so," I said.

"Why not?"

"She's kind of a flake. She has no eyebrows. I know women pluck their eyebrows and stuff, but still, I mean, there is like, nothing there. Every time I look her in the eyes it freaks me out. It's like I am looking into the eyes of a ghost. And besides, she always smells like Jolly Ranchers."

"Jolly Ranchers?"

"Yeah, Jolly Ranchers. You know, those candies that look like hard Jell-O."

"Oh candy," he yawned. "That could be perfume. My wife has candy perfume."

"Still, that doesn't make it right. She puts too much on and the smell is nauseating."

The phone jolted Esan. He scrambled to pick up the receiver, recited the code word and slammed the receiver down.

"Okay fine," Esan said. "Don't go out with her. Blow her off. What's the big deal? Just act like yourself, that should be enough to repel this women."

"I can't do that either. I'm failing electromagnetic and I need her to pass. The head of the Physics department said I was on his death watch. I think they want to give my spot to someone with a GPA above 2.0."

We sat there for a while, listening to the cars on the street.

"You're in a bit of a pickle. You can't just do nothing. You are going to have to reciprocate."

"Reciprocate! This thing cost sixteen dollars!" I swiped the chocolate box off the counter and jabbed the air around Esan's face with it. "This isn't Scarborough campus. These Mississauga people throw money around like a bad habit. If I start spending my money on chocolate boxes, I'm going to have to give up too many things I enjoy, like food, water and cigarettes! I need my money to live. If I start reciprocating, it'll start a vicious cycle. Not to mention the fact that this thing is a time bomb waiting to blow my personal life apart! I came to you because I don't want to reciprocate. You're the cheapest person I know. Help me out."

"All right. Let me think." Esan rubbed his temples and yawned.

"All right," I said. "That's cool, you think. I'm going upstairs to watch wrestling," I said as I dropped the remaining chocolate in Esan's huge mouth. As Esan gagged on the chocolate, I ran to the elevator. Wrestling started in a couple of minutes.

2:00 a.m.

I watched wrestling, confident that the adrenalin rush would keep me awake until at least 4:00 a.m. I came back down in the elevator and when the doors parted I stood horrified by what I saw.

Crap Lobby

Esan slouched asleep and a faint buzzing sounded everywhere at once and filled the lobby. Esan's head had fallen on the buzzer we used for the side door. The homeless guy I had rousted earlier squatted in the middle of the lobby, pants around his ankles. Faeces flowed freely onto the pristine marble floor from his bony behind.

"Hey! Excuse me...Excuse me...*Excuse me*!!? What are you doing!?" I yelled.

Esan shot upright and stumbled out of the chair in a confused stupor. The hobo ran out of the building with a turd between his legs as he pulled up his stained grey pants. I chased after him, but I didn't make it more than a couple of steps before I was slapped in the face by the scent wafting from the pile, a mixture of cheap liquor, sweat socks and raw sewage.

"Are you crazy? What's wrong with you?!" I screamed at Esan. "Look at this." I pointed to the large stool sample on the floor and coughed up phlegm.

"It smells like rancid barbecue," Esan said.

"Well, clean it up."

Esan glared at me.

"Fine. We'll just sit here and you can explain in the morning."

"Fine. I don't care."

"Neither do I."

"This is your fault! Clean it up."

"No way."

Seconds took hours to pass as we stood around, studiously avoiding looking at the shit pile.

"That's it!" I walked closer to ground zero and pointed. "I can't look at that for the rest of the shift! I don't care what you say. This is your fault. So if you're not going to clean it up at least put some pylons around it or go get some Lysol. I'm going home."

"This is not my fault. I didn't do that," Esan said.

I walked to my chair and pulled my coat off of the back of the cushioned aquamarine seat.

"You're leaving? You can't leave."

"Or what? We're going to get fired? We're already fired unless you clean that up. The clock is ticking."

"You're leaving me here by myself?" Esan moved his large frame between the door and me putting his chest in my face.

"Why? Are you going to do something about it?"

"No."

"Then let me pass."

Esan stepped to the right. I collected my things and left. I didn't expect Esan to clean up the mess. I walked out onto the sidewalk, scanned Yonge Street for a cab and put on my scarf as the windchill, which now turned the rain into snow, bit into my skin.

3:00 a.m.

I walked into my dank hole of a basement apartment, kicked the snow off my shoes and reached around for the light. My face felt numb and my ears stung. I closed the door behind me, flicked on the light and dropped my keys on the counter. There was no denying it—I was fucked. Not only had a bum shit in the lobby, I had left Esan alone to clean up the mess.

There was also no point in trying to sleep now. It was just past three in the morning and I had slept during the day to prepare for the night shift. I went to the fridge and opened the door. I had two options: Marla's cold spaghetti with watery sauce or a full bottle of Jack Daniels. I pulled out the Jack Daniels.

Crap Lobby

Cold whisky is just plain wrong, but there was nowhere else I could put it. Marla wanted it out of sight. She didn't like liquor just lying around, but she also hated cooking. The fridge served as our little compromise. I poured myself a double shot and drained it. As Jack warmed me up from the inside, I threw my jacket on the couch and trudged to the bedroom.

I stood by the bed and watched Marla's back rise and fall in the dark as she slept. I could see nothing else. I needed light, but I didn't want to wake her. I crept through the darkness to the lamp on my side of the bed—I didn't make it. I caught my foot on something and fell with a thud. On the way down I smacked my head on one of the wooden bedposts and broke my glasses.

"Oh, fuck off!" I said as quietly as I could, considering my pain. I would have lain there until morning but I wasn't tired enough to fall asleep and the whisky on my breath would give Marla another opportunity to lecture me about boozing.

When the throbbing in my head subsided, I stumbled my way up from among the remains of my glasses to the lamp. I turned the plastic knob and crawled back to the end of the bed. Anger rose inside me as I looked down at a pair of Marla's blue jeans, a pair of her socks, her blouse and a stack of undergarments piled up at the foot of the bed. Fragments of my broken glasses scattered around her clothes.

"Vile woman!" I whispered through gritted teeth.

I looked at Marla with the comforter pulled up to her neck, looked back down at her clothes on the ground beside her backpack and I had an epiphany. I peeled back the comforter and peeked underneath to see what she wore.

"Damnation!" I groaned.

Marla wore her ratty flannel pyjama bottoms and one of my shirts.

"Huh...What is it? What do you want?" Marla croaked and squinted at me.

"Nothing. You've already done enough. Go back to sleep."

The questions came quickly after that.

"What did I do? What happened to you? Why aren't you at work? Why are you bleeding?"

"A homeless guy shit in the lobby."

"What?"

"A homeless guy. He shit in the lobby. That's why I'm not at work. Just go back to sleep. I'll tell you in the morning."

"Then turn off that fucking light and do something about that cut. It looks nasty." Marla rolled over and went back to sleep.

I pulled off my socks and put my wallet and the golden chocolate box on the bedside table before I turned the lamp off.

"Oh, by the way, take off my shirt," I said.

"Wha??" She mumbled from the dark.

"Take off my shirt! What am I supposed to wear if you're wearing all my stuff?"

"This was in the hamper. You weren't going to wear it anyway. It's dirty."

"That's not the point. You wear my shirts and they get all warped. I look like I'm top heavy or something."

"Maybe you should buy baggier clothes then."

"Just take it off, woman."

"Fuck you." She pulled her pillow over her head.

I sighed and got up to leave the room. As I sidestepped Marla's pile of clothes, I felt a piece of jagged metal sink into the sole of my right foot.

Crap Lobby

As soon as I hopped out of the bedroom, I let out a girlish scream and slumped against the living room wall. I prepared to pull the piece of metal from my foot when a craggy voice yelled from the bedroom.

"Why won't you shut…the fuck…up!"

6:45 a.m.

We had no rubbing alcohol, so I went back to the fridge for the next best thing. I tied a Jack Daniels soaked towel around the two-inch tear in the bottom of my foot and held a Jack Daniels soaked towel to the gash above my right eye. Since I was in no condition to return the bottle to the fridge, I finished it off.

After I patched myself up, I sat at the dinner table, propped my wounded foot on another chair, smoked the half-pack of Camels Marla had left on the table and read a two-day-old *Toronto Sun* from Sunshine Girl to Sunshine Boy. In the darkness, the clock on the stove glowed six-something. I squinted, six fifty-something. I felt nauseous. I felt light-headed. I felt tired. I limped to the bedroom, hoping I could fall asleep before the sun came up.

Taking no chances, I probed with my feet before placing them firmly on the floor, climbed into bed and drifted into unconsciousness. It seemed like seconds before the alarm went off.

9:00 a.m.

The piercing *bleat! bleat!* of the alarm felt like an electric shock through my body. My heart pounded through my chest and my foot throbbed.

"Turn that thing off! Please turn it off."

We both had a habit of letting the alarm bleat until we fully awoke. Sunlight shone in my face. I was awake. Marla rolled over to face me.

"So why aren't you at work?" she asked.

"A homeless guy took a dump in the lobby."

"That's what you said last night, and it doesn't make any more sense today than it did last night."

I explained the misadventure with Esan, the homeless guy, the Ass Scratcher and the Ass Scratcher's luxurious office.

"And the cut?" she asked. "How did you get that cut? And by the way, you scream like a girl. What the hell was that for?"

"What was that for? What was that for? It was for the glasses I smashed and the piece of metal I stuck in my foot because you're too lazy to put your shit in the goddamn hamper. I tripped over that pile of garbage you left there." I opened my hand towards the heap of clothes on the ground.

"How stupid do you have to be to trip on a pile of clothes that big?"

"It was dark. I couldn't see."

"What are you, a fucking moron? Turn on a light."

"You were sleeping. You would have told me to turn the light off, which you did anyway. And by the way, take off my shirt."

"Fuck. you," she said, as she moved in closer and turned my head to look at the cut above my eye. "And your foot. Let's see your foot."

She pulled the towel off my foot, but before she could look at it, I rolled on top of her. She smiled as I pulled her close and kissed her. Our tongues touched as she pushed me over and rolled on top of me. Then something caught her attention. Her face became cold and hard. She scowled. Before I could react she pulled her tongue out of my mouth and clamped her teeth on my tongue.

Crap Lobby

"At'saaht?"

"Huh? Huh?"

"Aaht!" she growled. Yanking my tongue, she motioned with her head toward the golden chocolate box and the pink envelope. She bit down hard before she let my tongue loose.

"Ah yoo crazy! Gawd zzammit!" I yelled, bringing my hand to my mouth. I ran my fingers lightly over the impressions Marla's front teeth had made on my tongue. When I pulled my fingers out of my mouth, traces of blood stained the tips.

"What is that?!" Marla's voice cracked as she yelled at me.

"Oh that." My mind strained to come up with something, anything. "That's for you."

"What? You think this is funny?" Marla's long brown hair fell forward in to her face, which had reddened, as she continued to rage. "It's from that eyebrowless woman isn't it?"

"Well, yeah...but—"

"You're such a whore! You get your head turned by any woman with a box of chocolates! First I'm going to beat the shit out of this woman, then I'm going to beat the fuck out of you! You little bastard! So how are they?"

"What?"

"The chocolates! How are they?"

"I don't know. Esan ate them all."

"Sure he did! Skank-whore!"

I realized that as long as she was on top of me, I was never going to win the argument. So I decided to go for a draw. I looked up into her brown eyes, pierced her deathstare and reasoned with her.

"What do you think? I'm doing something with this woman?"

"What the hell am I supposed to think? Why are you accepting gifts from her?"

"I'm flunking electromagnetic. What am I supposed to do? I need her!"

"So she's smart?"

"At electromagnetic. Smarter than I am anyway. All I've been able to figure out after three-and-a-half months is that $v=ir$. I don't even know what v, i and r stand for, just that $v=ir$."

"And her big tits have absolutely nothing to do with it."

I regretted piercing her deathstare. I would have given anything to look past her, through her, or away from her.

"Yeah, I looked in on one of your classes," she said. "I saw this woman."

"Me? No! I'm not a breast man…I'm an eyebrow man. And if you saw her you know she doesn't have any eyebrows."

Marla looked at me and shook her head.

"You really don't think much of me, do you?" she said.

"I admit I never really noticed eyebrows before, but after looking at her I realize how important eyebrows are in the makeup of how a person looks." I rambled, hoping to stumble onto something.

Marla looked at the pink envelope. "What does the card say?"

"It's a birthday card."

"A birthday card? It's fucking December."

"You see I—"

"That's it," she interrupted. "You're going to tell her today that you're engaged and put a stop to this nonsense."

"Think about this. You and me, we can handle this. We know there's nothing there. She's a nut! It doesn't matter that I already have a girlfriend, she's got some kind of persecution complex. It's all about her. Plus she smells like candy and she has no eyebrows and she lives at Jane and Woolner. Have you ever been to Jane and Woolner? It's a fucking war zone! I mean it's worse than Scarborough. Even I'm

Crap Lobby

afraid to go there. If I blow her off then I have to study on my own and I'll fail this exam. Esan was supposed to help me out, but he's an idiot and he let a homeless guy shit in the lobby."

We said nothing.

She spoke first. "How do you know where she lives?"

"Will you please look at the big picture? Now can you handle it please? Do it for me."

"Sure. Fine. I can handle it." She rolled out of bed.

"Oh, come on! Don't be like that! Don't tell me I'm not going to hit it because of the eyebrowless woman!"

"Don't worry. You were never going to hit it. You smell like a gin mill, you wrapped my bath towel around your bleeding foot and you smoked my cigarettes. Didn't you?"

I said nothing.

"Exactly," she continued. "Get out of bed and get dressed. We're going to the hospital. You need stitches."

"Get dressed?" I groaned aloud. "I never took off my uniform."

10:15 a.m.

Marla sat hunched with her elbows on the kitchen table. She ate Cap'n Crunch and read the horoscope section of the old *Toronto Sun*. Her spoon clinked against her bowl as she crunched her cereal. She looked beautiful. She confused me and annoyed me and she loved me unconditionally and I had angered her. I stood close behind her and looked down at the newspaper.

"Reading the horoscopes?"

She half-grunted.

I took that as permission to continue. "They say the horoscopes are based on the planets. That they can tell your fortune by how Venus and Neptune are aligned with the stars or something like that."

Marla half-grunted again and shrugged her shoulder.

I was sinking fast.

"When I was a kid, my dad and I would sit outside at night and look at the stars sometimes. We tried to find the constellations and stuff, you know, like the big dipper or something. We never did."

"I wouldn't know about that," she said. "Stars never really caught my attention."

"In the city you can't really see them. We were in Saudi Arabia then. No lights, not like here anyway, you know. It seemed like the sky was jammed with stars, that there were too many. Maybe you and I can take a trip somewhere and look at the stars."

Her voice softened. "You should probably go with your dad. He would appreciate it more than I would."

"It wouldn't be the same. Besides, it's too late for my dad and me. I think the gap grew between him and me because when the opportunity came up for us to put things right we handled it all wrong." I paused. "I left so many things unsaid." I put my hand on Marla's right shoulder. "You are the most important thing in my life."

She leaned back in her chair, brought her left hand up to her shoulder and intertwined her fingers with mine.

"I know you would never do anything with that woman," she said.

I leaned down and kissed her hair.

"I would never do anything to hurt you," I said. "Now come on, we've gotta get out of here." I limped to get my coat as Marla left to start the car.

10:30 a.m.

By the time I climbed into in the car, I had been up sixteen of the last eighteen hours. I dozed off. As soon as I had fallen asleep, Marla poked me awake and thrust her cellular into my face.

"Work," she said.

Work was all she had to say.

I yawned and smiled into the phone as I prepared to speak. My continued employment as a defender of empty office buildings depended on how I answered this phone call. I put the receiver to my ear. "Hey Alex, how's it going?"

"What in God's name were you two doing? How could you let a homeless guy shit in the lobby?"

He talked, but I stopped listening. I realised the futility of trying to save my job. I felt bad about leaving Esan all alone so I decided to do something noble.

"Well you see, I fell asleep on the buzzer and—"

"I already know what happened. Esan told me. Do you know what makes it worse? Between the two of you, you couldn't catch the guy! You know what makes it even worse than that? Neither of you bothered to clean it up! Do you know what Esan did? He put a garbage can over it! And that was only after people walked in and saw it. Did he think the garbage can was going to contain the smell? Do you know what it's like to go to work and see a pile of shit there?"

"Must be pretty bad, I guess."

"Pretty bad?" Alex said.

I couldn't tell if Alex thought I was being a smartass or if he just thought I was a moron.

"You're suspended," he said. "If and when you're reinstated you'll be reassigned. And you better hope and pray I don't send you to Scarborough Town Centre."

I pushed the "end" button and placed the phone on the dashboard.

"Well?" Marla asked.

"I've more or less been fired."

"That's a real shame. You know what I've decided?" she spoke in a malicious tone she used when she wanted to fuck with me. "I've decided I'm going to tell you my little secret. I wasn't going to say anything for a couple more days. But after last night, if I have to handle the eyebrowless woman you're going to handle my little secret. You wanna hear it?"

"Not really, no."

"Too bad," she snapped.

I readied myself for a confession involving a moment of passion between her and one of the faceless guys in one of those inane poli-sci classes she took.

"After you get stitched up," she said, "we're going shopping in the pharmacy. You know what we're shopping for?"

"Not particularly," I said.

She had caught me off guard. I thought we had made up.

"Home pregnancy tests! Why? Because I'm almost a week late, that's why. I would have got you a box of chocolates, but who wants chocolate when you could have a fucking baby? Happy birthday, asshole."

"You made your point," I said. "I'll blow her off and study on my own."

Marla glowered but said nothing as she drove. I stared out the passenger-side window at the few cars scattered across the vast parking lot of the Erin Mills Town Centre and thought about the possibility that today could be even worse than last night.

One Night in a Basement Apartment

I read it for the millionth time. *Dear Sultan: People change. I've changed...I love my dad...I felt like you made me choose between you and him and ultimately I am my father's daughter.*

This last line was the kicker. It was as far as I could read. I crumpled up the cliché-filled note she had written on her yellow stationery with flowery borders and tossed it out the bedroom door into the hallway.

The envelope lying on the fake marble counter caught my eye when I got in from a night class at Erindale. I pulled the note from the envelope and read as I walked into the bedroom. After I had read it the first time I pitched my coat onto the bed and yanked open both of her night table drawers, slid open the closet door and flung apart the flimsy wooden doors of the wardrobe.

The silk blouse I had bought for Marla from Holt Renfrew, the blouse that she never wore but kept at the front of the closet because even though she hated it she knew it was expensive and I had put some effort into selecting it and that was when we instituted the rule that we would only buy each other clothes if the other person was there. She kept three pairs of shoes in a corner of the wardrobe. Marla never had the big inventory of shoes like other women. She had a worn-in pair of white Reebok runners that she only ever wore when we played tennis that one time. She had long leather shaft boots that accentuated her legs when we went to clubs or out somewhere special together and a new black pair of Nike running shoes that she would wear to school in a few weeks when spring came and the snow fully melted. I had convinced her that white running shoes looked ugly with blue jeans and now she would only wear her old black Nike running shoes to school, but the sole on the black Nike running shoes had started to peel from the rest of the shoe. I had bought her a new pair from the Bay a few weeks ago and she had pulled them out of the box and brown paper wrapping and stuck them in the corner with the other shoes, waiting for spring, so she could wear them and toss the old pair which leaked when she walked in puddles anyway. She used one drawer in the wardrobe for her underwear, a mess of white bras and white panties and the one black sports bra that she could always find because it contrasted with everything else.

It was gone. All of it was gone.

Blue phosphorus light radiated from behind Mississauga Transit and George Brown advertisements and flooded the brown plastic seats and the black rubber floors of the 13 Clarkson bus in a cold eerie blue. Thundershowers pounded outside.

The lone passenger, I sat in silence and stared out the window at darkness. Fields of unkept grass stretched into the horizon and pushed up against the concrete of the parkway on one side. Square blocks of stone-grey townhouses lined the other side. Droplets hit the windowpane, streamed down, merged into each other, picked up speed and disappeared. The bus turned and the window now reflected empty blue-tinged, brown plastic seats.

The only vehicle on the road, the bus navigated the curved roads around the Erin Mills Town Centre and turned onto Glen Erin Drive. I grabbed the pole in front of me, pulled myself up and walked towards the driver. His eye darted up to the mirror, then back to the road as he turned onto Glen Erin Drive.

"You getting off?" he said.

"Yeah." I turned to face him as the front doors slid and separated. I felt cold air and moisture.

Our eyes met. The corners of my mouth turned up. He smiled and we both nodded. "You have a good night," I said.

"You too, son. You too."

It was half past eleven on a Sunday night and all the important people here were already asleep. They rested for Monday morning. For me and Mr. Bus Driver, today was still today. We understood.

I bounded down the steps into stinging rain. I waited for the bus to pull away before I crossed the empty street. Water pelted my leather jacket and in seconds soaked through my shirt and jeans as I walked along Glen Erin Drive and lumbered up the driveway of a large grey house. I took the concrete path to the left of the double garage—not the brick pathway on the right that lead to the front porch. The concrete path led to the basement entrance: a concrete staircase leading down into a small, concrete-encased pit.

Water covered the bottom of the pit. A black rubber mat lay at the foot of a plain grey door. The bottom of the wooden door warped where water lapped against it. Dim light glowed from the rectangular windows of the door.

I descended into the pit, dug into the pocket of my blue jeans, felt for the keys that had burrowed into my right thigh for the last two hours and I pulled up old soggy GO Train tickets, wet TTC tickets and wetter Mississauga Transit tickets. I got a hold of the keys and the door opened. I pulled back. Marla stood far enough inside the doorway to avoid the rain. "Hurry up and get inside," she said. "You're soaked."

I walked in. Water from around the sides of the rubber mat followed me inside. Marla slammed the door, tiptoed away from the puddles and stepped onto a damp towel crumpled near the kitchen counter. With her bare foot, Marla dragged the towel towards the puddles and swiped at the water. When the towel had soaked up the water she pushed it up against the foot of the door.

"Who designed this house?" I said.

I tossed my jacket onto the counter. Water rolled off the worn black leather onto the fake marble counter top. "I've got to talk to Jay about putting a rubber strip or something in the doorway."

"We can worry about that later. Get out of those clothes. You're going to catch a cold or something."

"Or something."

I marched into the bedroom and peeled off wet clothes along the way. I threw them into a pile in the corner by the closet, put on a pair of track pants and collapsed onto the bed. My eyes closed and my mind drifted.

"Wake up!" Marla yelled as she walked into the room and threw a towel at me. "You're soaking the mattress."

The towel hit me in the face. I shot upright at the sound of her voice and whipped the towel back at her.

"What the fuck!" I screamed back. "One minute. One god damned minute." I sat on the edge of the bed and ran my hands through my hair. Water dripped down my back and I looked at her out of the corner of my eye.

One Night in a Basement Apartment

I looked up at Marla. I looked at her, really looked at her, for the first time in two weeks. Marla stood frozen in the bedroom doorway. She blinked back tears. Marla wore black lycra tights and an old white T-shirt that had been washed too many times, leaving it shrunken and frayed around the edges. Locks of her long curly brown hair fell onto her solemn face.

"Sorry," I said. It came out soft and almost inaudible. "It's just that fucking job and having to stay with my parents. It's killing me."

Marla walked over, sat down beside me and soaked water out of my hair with the towel. I jerked my head towards her. She squealed and laughed as pellets of water hit her face.

"You're letting your hair grow out," she said as she ran her left hand through my wet, curled, tangled black knots of hair.

"Not really. I just haven't had time to cut it."

"You don't have time for anything. If the job is that bad why don't you just quit?"

"I can't. Need the money."

"What do you mean you can't? Ever since you started working at SkyDome we never see each other. What's the point of working a job to pay the rent and move out of your parents' house if you're going to live there while you work the job?"

"My parents' house is closer. I can't get to SkyDome from Mississauga for seven o'clock."

"So stay here and drive my car."

"We can't afford to pay for the gas and parking. Besides I don't want to give that limey cock sucker the satisfaction of seeing me quit. Peter's so tight with money I want to see the look on his face when he hands me that severance cheque. You know he's selling Amway products now. It's bad enough I gotta take orders from him, now I have to listen to him try and recruit people into his cult."

"If you can't stay here, what are you doing here now? You have work in like seven hours."

"I took the next two days off. When I heard your voice on the phone you didn't sound too good. I was worried about you...sorta missed you."

"I sort of missed you too," Marla said. "Sort of." She pulled her hand out of my hair and pulled her feet up onto the bed.

I rummaged in the nightstand drawer and pulled out a green board and a metal lock box. I sat on the bed, opened up the lockbox and pulled out a dime bag of weed.

"You know," I said as I poured the grass out of the plastic bag and into a shot glass. "I'm thinking that maybe you're right, I might just stay here. I mean, it's pretty bad at my parents' house. It's not even my dad cause he doesn't talk to me anyway—it's everybody else. I don't need their crap after twelve hours of dealing with that Amway-schilling motherfucker."

"What happened to 'it costs too much money'?"

"No amount of money is worth my sanity." I took a pair of scissors from the lockbox and snipped the dried, greenish-brown bits of weed. "It'll make it easier for us to see each other anyway." I pulled out a Zig-Zag paper and poured pieces of grass onto the paper. I rolled up the paper and licked one end of it before sealing the joint. "I mean whenever you can get away from your parents, you know I'll be here," I said, twisting one end shut.

"Actually, I've been staying here for about a week," Marla said. "That's why I called you. They kicked me out."

"Kicked you out? Is this about me?"

"They know about everything."

"What? You told them?"

One Night in a Basement Apartment

"They're not stupid and they were going to figure it out anyway—so I just told them." Marla's voice quivered and her breathing became ragged. "Papa, he called me a Nigger lover." Marla looked away from me. Tears rolled down her cheeks. "You wouldn't believe the things he said, Sultan." She sniffled and wiped her nose. "I can't believe that was my father."

My body tensed at the word. Nigger. I mulled the word over. "I'm sorry," I said. "I know you got along good with your family." I regretted the words as they came out of my mouth. What the hell was I apologizing for? Not being a white guy? This man I had never met had made my life more complicated. I now had two people to support instead of one and for the first time since I was a child I felt ashamed of being a brown man.

I waited for Marla to say something. She said nothing. I tried to relieve the tension. "I guess I can't quit that job now, huh?" I laughed.

Marla's body racked. Tears flowed down her face.

"I'm so sorry. I know how much you hate that job and now you have to stay there because of me."

I brushed her hair out of her face and wiped her tears with my thumb. I knew what I was about to say next and I knew what it meant. I felt trapped and I hated the old bastard even more.

"Don't be sorry. You didn't do anything wrong. My contract at SkyDome is up in a month anyway. I wasn't going to quit. Your friends and your brother, they think the same way as the old man?"

She nodded.

I held her close and lay back on the bed. "I guess we have everything bet on each other, don't we? You know I'm not even a Nigger. I'm a Paki. There's a huge difference between a Nigger and a Paki."

Marla snorted out a laugh, took the joint from me and lit it. "I'm aware of the differences between a Nigger and a Paki."

"That's like calling a Dago a Polock. How would your old man like it if I went over to his house and started calling him a Polock?"

"Papa is actually German and even if you didn't call him a Polock he wouldn't like it if you went over to his house. But I see your point."

As we passed the joint between us, the fluorescent light flickered and the gloomy room filled with the sweet stench of marijuana.

Marla hacked and coughed as she tried to hold the burning smoke in her lungs. She looked at me as I took in a drag and smiled. The radio played softly and Paul McCartney sang *Let it Be*. His voice slowed to a dull drone as the weed kicked in and I smiled back at her and waited for her to tell me that she wasn't sorry about getting kicked out by her dad and I wanted her to say she didn't regret the way things had turned out and she said nothing. We finished the joint. Marla lay her head on my chest and slept.

I sat on the edge of my bed and rubbed the light stubble on my jaw. My eyes locked on the empty storage spaces. The empty spaces, smelling faintly of her perfume, stared back at me. I read and reread Marla's note for the next hour, as I tried to figure out exactly why she had left. *People change. I've changed…ultimately I am my father's daughter.* I didn't know what made me angrier, that after three years—and everything we had been through—I didn't merit a face-to-face goodbye, or that I wasn't important enough to merit at least one original sentence. The letter was a mix of soap-opera dialogue, clichés from old black-and-white movies and the unmistakable fact that her racist father meant more to her than I did and ever could. I stopped trying to convince myself that the way it sounded on the page wasn't what she meant—because I knew it was when I hurled the letter out into the hall.

I leaned towards my black trench coat and pulled a clear plastic sandwich bag of powdery white crystals from the inside pocket. I undid the green twist-tie and with slow precision poured the crystals onto the black lacquer finish of the bedside table. I opened the drawer and pulled an old playing card, the jack of spades, from inside the drawer.

The small, white pile sparkled against the black surface. Soft light glowed down from the bedside lamp inches away. I cut the pile of crystals with my jack of spades and pushed a small helping to one side. I sliced the bigger pile into two. Using the jack I shoved the piles into three crooked lines. I plugged my right nostril with my thumb, leaned in towards the closest line and snorted it straight into my brain.

I hunched over the end of the bed, elbows on my knees with my head between my legs and the room blurred, the corners of the room where walls and ceiling met rounded and melted into each other and the room felt fuzzy and hot as self-doubt, self-pity, sadness and fear mutated into pleasure. My eyes watered. I pulled my glasses off and dropped them in the drawer and my right arm felt wooden and heavy as I pushed the drawer shut.

I plugged my right nostril and inhaled the second line. My head jerked as the crystals hit my brain. My nose ran. I tried to snort the snot back into my nose. My body felt dense and my head heavy, attached to my body but not a part of it. I fell back onto the bed, stared at the ceiling and coughed as snot ran back up my nose and down my throat.

I gazed at the rough, textured drywall of the ceiling and watched it dissolve into a lake of white liquid that rippled as I thought about our last fight. I fought to keep my eyes open as I thought about how she had carefully taken everything that was hers, but had left the sandwich maker, the water filter and anything else that was ours. My belts still looped around the wooden pole of the closet and my dress shirts still hung on the pole that ran across the wardrobe.

I didn't check the rest of the bedroom. I would find all my things where I had them that morning. Marla had picked most of my clothes out for me. Before I met her I wore jeans and sweatshirts, but for her I dressed up. I liked the compliments I received on my new look. Who was going to pick out my clothes now? I thought about her underwear again. Did other women fold their bras and panties or was Marla just lazy? It seemed like a pointless exercise, like a man folding his underwear, but with women you never know what's pointless. I thought I knew a lot about women, but I didn't, I actually knew a lot about one woman and nothing about the species as a whole and I was scared Marla wasn't coming back.

I had held her hand as I sat beside her bed in a wooden chair that hurt my back, in an antiseptic, beige hospital room. Numb and silent, we waited for a doctor to come back and tell us what we already knew. Marla had lost the baby. The doctor questioned us. Did we know she was pregnant? Yes and no. Was there anyone that we wanted to call? Not particularly. On the way home from the hospital we argued in the car about why she hadn't told me she was pregnant.

Marla had been in a dark mood since the miscarriage. Sullen, angry, reflective, she spoke rarely and yelled at the refrigerator when it broke.

Two months ago, I had found her sprawled across the bed. Blood stained the bedspreads and the towels and she looked so pale I shudder every time I remember.

Marla sipped from a tumbler of Chivas as she picked at her macaroni dinner. Even by our standards, she was drinking more than usual.

"I've been talking to my mom," she said from across the table. Marla looked at her plate and played with her fork in the curled pasta.

"I know," I said.

Normally she slept beside me, but for the last two weeks I lay in bed alone. One night a nightmare jolted me awake. My skin felt pasty with cold sweat. I heard her voice from the hallway but I couldn't make out the words. I lay in bed and listened. When she came back, I pretended to sleep. Some nights I listened for hours.

"You didn't say anything?"

"I thought that it was good—that you had somebody to talk to. I wish you hadn't kept it from me. But I figured you would tell me when you were ready."

"It's good to have somebody to talk to…especially since you're not around as much."

"What do you mean not around?"

"With the job and school and—"

"I go to school less than you do and I quit the job to spend more time with you."

"You were suspended."

"And when they brought me back, I quit."

"You quit because they sent you to that fucking hellhole in Scarborough instead of a downtown office building. That doesn't count. I mean, when do we spend time together outside of this fucking hole in the ground?" she asked. "Tell me, when do we ever spend time together outside of this hole in the ground?" Marla paused and chose her words. "I want you to come with me somewhere."

"Anywhere. I was thinking maybe we should have taken a trip after the whole thing anyway. Take some time to put it behind us. Where do you want to go?"

"Church. I want you to come with me to church."

"Anywhere but there. You got a second choice?"

"This isn't funny!"

"Believe me, I don't think this is funny at all."

"Why not?"

"I don't want to go to church."

"Why not?"

"I can't. Knowing who I am, I just can't. That's all."

"My parents. They want to meet you. My father finally realizes I'm not just dicking around with you. You're saying you can't do this. Even for me."

"I'll meet him—just not in church. I have a father too, Marla."

"You hate the man."

"I don't hate him. He's just old, a product of his time. Besides, I don't want to go to church."

Marla glared at me. I caught her glance and she looked away. She stretched her hand out mechanically for the tumbler and took a long pull of Chivas that drained the glass.

"What?! Is it so hard for you to believe that I have some principles? That I might not feel right in a church?"

"No."

"You don't believe me, do you? You think this has to do with your old man. Marla, I've never met the man. This has nothing to do with him."

"Okay, fine."

"Say it! Say that you believe me."

"I believe you Sultan."

We ate the rest of our meal in silence.

My eyelids felt pulled down by weights and I thought about nothing. I felt nothing. I lay motionless, emotionless and thoughtless. My eyes flickered open, then closed.

Sometime later, I felt warmth caress my face as beams of light from the sunrise crept across the room from the small window and violated the dankness of my basement apartment. I raked my nails across my stomach, stripped off my shirt and trekked to the washroom.

My stomach churned and my head throbbed. Hot burning spew surged up my throat. Vomit exploded out of my mouth and hit the side of the white toilet seat, splattered into the toilet and against the opaque plastic shower curtain. Pain ripped through my stomach and I dropped to one knee. Every breath I took burned as air passed over the vomit residue that coated the back of my throat. Acid burned my stomach as my lungs expanded.

I doubled over the toilet and the smell triggered torrents. My empty stomach collapsed on itself. Vomiting became dry retching.

I lay down on the tile until the spasms stopped. The cool tiles soothed my burning face. When the spasms stopped, I grasped the doorknob and pulled myself up to the sink, turned on the hot water tap and splashed hot water on my face. The water burned my skin red. I looked down at my hands. My red palms throbbed from the water when I reached for a razor blade. Steam rose from the sink and I concentrated to see through it and look at my jawlines in the mirror. I started to shave. If I hurried I could clean myself up and still get to Erindale to see Marla before her nine o'clock political science class.

Tattoo—Blow Job Story

Two Days Ago

All I could see was the red glow of the tip of my cigarette. I lay flat on my back in a cloud of smoke in my darkened room. My left arm hung over the side of the bed and a Player's Light cigarette wedged between my fingers. My brother Kish opened the door, and I squinted as bright light from the hallway shone through the nicotine haze and fell onto my face.

"Hey man, phone call for you. Some chippie." He stood in the doorway with his face contorted as he waved smog away. I exhaled another cloud of smoke, sat up, brought the pager in my right hand closer to my face and looked at the grey screen.

"Was the number 555-3589?" I said.

"Not sure, but that sounds familiar."

"Tell her I'm out. You don't know when I'll be back."

"Maybe you should tell her yourself. You could use practice talking to real people," he said.

"Maybe you should mind your own business. Either tell her I'm out or tell her I can't come to the phone. I honestly don't care which."

"Calm down old man, you know eventually the suckass gotta know. But I'll tell her you're out."

"Thank you."

"You're welcome." Kish closed the door.

I fell back onto the bed and fixated on the red glow of the tip of my cigarette as I smoked in the dark.

This Morning

I woke up with a jackhammer throbbing in my head. I tried to sit up and a wave of nausea pushed me back as the chicken gyro I had for dinner last night bucked and thrashed in my stomach. I knew I wasn't at home—everything was pink. The ceiling, the walls, even the curtains, all of it pink. I steadied myself until the nausea passed, and I turned towards Virginia.

Already awake, she lay on her side, watching me. The bed sheet fell away from her body and revealed bare breasts as she propped herself up with her elbow, leaned towards me and smiled. She ran her hand through my hair and rubbed the back of my neck with her thumb and index finger.

"You okay?" she asked.

"Yeah, I'm fine."

"You look like you're about to throw up."

"It's nothing I can't handle. I've been worse. How much of it do you remember?"

"Most of it. Almost all, actually," she said.

I didn't know what else to say. I cleared my throat and tried to remember post-sex conversation etiquette.

"Don't worry. You were fine," she added.

Was she being funny? Was she just trying to make conversation? It hadn't even occurred to me that I might have been anything below "fine." I probed for more information.

Tattoo—Blow Job Story

"Fine, huh. Just fine?" I asked, disappointed that this was the most probing question I could come up with.

She laughed and kissed my cheek.

"Maybe a little better than fine. I'll get you a glass of water. You're dehydrated."

Virginia wrapped the yellow bed sheet around her petite body and waddled out the door and down the stairs, towards the kitchen. When I heard the kitchen tap, I leapt out of bed and looked around for my clothes. I scanned the pink carpet and found most of my clothes at the foot of the bed. My pants stuck out from under the corner of the bed.

I put them on and went down to the kitchen, a tiny nook by the front door of her condo. My feet felt cold when I stepped onto the plastic tile of the kitchen floor from the plush carpet of the living room. Goose bumps dotted my arms.

Virginia handed me a glass of water.

"Thanks," I said. I took a small sip and set the glass on the counter. I didn't want to drink water. I wanted to make a graceful exit.

"You're cold," she said. Virginia sauntered over to me and rubbed my arms until the goosebumps disappeared. I moved my icy hands into her warm armpits. She flinched and pulled her arms in, heating my hands. She moved her hands to my chest and rubbed my right pectoral. "I love this tattoo," she purred.

I pushed my fingers between the bed sheet and her skin, loosening the knot she had tied underneath her armpit.

"I didn't believe you when you said that you had a tattoo. You look so...." she searched for a word.

"Nerdy," I volunteered while I tried to avoid vomiting all over her.

"No, not nerdy. You just don't seem like the type. That's all. This thing must drive the girls wild."

The thing she referred to, of course, was the tattoo—more specifically, a picture of the Joker, arch enemy of Batman, etched into my chest. I had the tattoo done when I was sixteen, an alternative to mugging an eighty-year-old woman for her welfare cheque as part of an initiation ritual. As for driving the girls wild, Marla never liked it. She always said that it looked garish but that it "suited my personality," and until last night Marla was the only woman I had ever slept with.

The tattoo had fascinated Virginia from the moment I mentioned it. I had brought it up in a desperate attempt to jump start our date—up to that point one giant awkward pause broken up by bits of small talk. She finally badgered me into showing her the tattoo in the lobby of her apartment building and invited me up, for what turned out to be several drinks, before I could even tuck my shirt back in.

"I honestly haven't given it a second thought," I said. I pulled the knot apart and looked down at Virginia's naked body as the bed sheet crumpled on the floor around her. "I've had this thing for so long that I don't pay any special attention to it anymore." My hands glided down her back, and I kissed her neck.

"You should," she moaned. Her body suddenly tensed. "I almost forgot." She gently moved my hands off of her backside. "Look, I have to get Shauna up for school. If you want to use the shower—"

Every instinct of self-preservation kicked in at the mention of her ten-year-old daughter and every instinct of self-preservation told me to get out of that house.

"Actually, you know what? I've got to get going, like right now. I've got an eight-thirty class."

"You can be late. At least eat something. You need your strength."

There are a lot of things I don't know. But what I did know is that I didn't want to have breakfast with the girl I had spent the night fucking and make small talk with her daughter.

"It's my photography class," I stammered. "I'm doing badly so I have to be there. I really should get going. You should, too. I'll see you at school." I kissed Virginia again and watched her body jiggle as I climbed the stairs behind her. I got dressed and left before her daughter spotted me.

Right Now

"You got laid, didn't you?" Kish said over the phone.

Instead of going to my photography class, I had bought a coffee and sat at a desk in the newsroom of the Journalism Program reading the *National Post*.

"What are you talking about?" I whispered to Kish on the phone.

"I didn't say that."

"Of course you got laid. You didn't come home last night."

"I had work to do at school."

"Don't hold out on me, man. The suckass gotta know."

"I can't talk now, but let's just say I got the grand tour of Virginia and I saw a little bit of South Carolina too, if you know what I mean."

Kish snickered on the other end of the line.

Mark walked into the newsroom from the far door and came towards me.

"Bring me a set of clothes if you're coming downtown," I said to Kish. "I got dressed in a hurry and I forgot to put on my underwear. I got to go." I hung up the phone before he could laugh at me, and I swivelled in my chair to face Mark.

Mark Atkinson was one of my smarter colleagues in my new Journalism Program. He shuffled towards me and smiled.

"How's it going, Sultan?" He stood over me where I sat at the desk with feet up, holding my newspaper.

"It's going really good," I said.

"Were you in class today?"

"No."

"Why are you smiling?"

"What?"

"Why are you smiling?"

"I'm not smiling."

"Yes you are. You're smiling. Ear to ear."

"So what? I'm not allowed to smile? It's nothing."

"You never smile. So what happened to you?"

"Nothing."

"You got laid last night, didn't you?"

"Man, get out of here."

Mark shuffled behind me, slid some papers inside the assignment drop box by the door, then opened the door.

"Everybody is in the lounge. Let's go. I want details."

"Details of what?" Aaron, another journalism colleague, walked into the newsroom and fed the drop box.

"Sultan got laid last night." Mark smiled.

Aaron grinned and nodded. "Oh yeah? That's awesome."

"I don't know what you're talking about," I said.

"Look at that grin," Mark said.

"You got laid and it was awesome," Aaron said. "Now we need details."

Tattoo—Blow Job Story

"You're both vultures. Leave me alone. I have to go to the bathroom."

"We'll be waiting." They filed out the door.

I sipped my coffee and read the sports section of the *Post*, while I tried to figure out how to tell them I had sex without telling them that I had sex with Virginia from the Radio and Television Program down the hall.

"You weren't in class today," a woman's voice said from behind me.

I recognised the voice as Fariah's. She had tracked me down.

"I had class today?"

"Photography at eight-thirty."

"What do I need to go to that for? I'm failing anyway."

"And what about me? You don't need me either. For two weeks you barely said anything to me. Now you're just avoiding me altogether."

"What are you talking about? I—" I realised a second too late that I smirked as I spoke.

She came around in front of me and pushed my feet off the table. Tears filled her eyes.

"This is funny to you!" she yelled.

Journalism students stopped and looked at us. They glanced away and pretended they were not listening.

I stood up and whispered, "Why don't we do this somewhere more private? How about this afternoon at—"

"Not this afternoon! Right now!" she said.

I opened my hand towards the door. "After you."

I followed her out the door, down the hall and outside to the parking lot. The frigid wind blew through my thin shirt and dress pants and reminded me that I had left my boxers underneath Virginia's bed. I jammed my hands deep into my pockets.

"So what's going on, Sultan? What? You can't talk to me?"

"What are you talking about? You called me out here."

"You're unbelievable." She shook her head.

"Look, Fariah, I'm sorry about this. It's just that you were so enthusiastic about everything and—"

"You weren't?"

"Not exactly."

"What about that night at Sharx?"

I couldn't put this off any longer. As Kish would have pointed out, the suckass gotta know.

"I don't think there was anything there. It was just head, and you were so nonchalant about it."

"So all you wanted was a blowjob?"

"Like I said, you were so nonchalant." I felt the dried gel caked into my hair. "I didn't think it would mean that much to you."

"And everything you said was a lie?"

"You know that's not fair. I didn't really say anything."

"Fair?" Tears streamed down her cheeks. "You string me along for weeks while you're doing Virginia?"

"What the hell are you talking about?"

"You had sex with Virginia last night."

"What are you talking about? No, of course not."

"Take off your shirt."

"What?"

"I heard Virginia in the washroom talking about a tattoo on your chest."

"Look at me. Do I look like someone who would have a tattoo? Think about this for a second."

Tattoo—Blow Job Story

She stared at me.

"You are the biggest pile of shit," she said. "Actually," she looked down at my groin, "You are the smallest—"

"Whatever. Let's just leave right now before we start saying things."

She ripped the door open and stalked inside. "Don't worry, I would never give you the satisfaction."

I pulled a Player's Light from my shirt pocket and lit it up. The cigarette dangled from my mouth as I shivered. I crossed my arms against the cold. I knew that I should feel bad about what I had just done. I felt only emptiness. I figured Fariah couldn't tell anybody I was an asshole without mentioning that she gave me head.

I thought about Virgina, looked down at the right side of my chest and thought about my boxer shorts under Virginia's bed.

I let out a wisp of smoke and wondered what Marla did last night.

Jennifer Lee

JENNIFER LEE, born in Ajax, Ontario, in 1975, to parents who had emigrated from Taiwan in the 1960s, graduated from the University of Toronto with a specialist in English and a minor in Environmental Studies. Following her graduating year, Lee spent a year in Beijing, China, teaching and improving her fluency in Mandarin. She currently works as a writer/editor for an environmental organization in Toronto.

The Red-Brick Path

Every so often, I catch a smell of Taiwan. I don't know whether it's Karen's Body Shop dewberry-scented perfume or the greasy Peking ducks that hang in the windows of Chinese restaurants in downtown Toronto.

The summer I turned twenty, after my first year at the University of Toronto, I got into a Chinese-Canadian Overseas Exchange Program at North Ocean University in Taipei, Taiwan. I boarded Air Canada flight 018 with my high school friend, Karen, to begin a six-week study tour. With one hundred and fifty other Chinese-Canadian-born students, we prepared to experience a culture we knew only through Chinese restaurants, Chinatown and our parents' stories.

Three days after we arrived in Taipei, Karen and I made friends with four other students from Scarborough, a suburb of Toronto: Michael, Tim, Tina and Nancy. We wore socks with velcro sandals, long T-shirts and jean shorts. We didn't look like the local women who wore silk skirts and blouses or the local men with their white undershirts and dress pants. With backpacks, cameras and water bottles, all six of us hiked down Gao Shong Main Street, the most congested street in Taipei. Cars, mopeds, delivery trucks and bicycles filled the four-lane, cracked-cement main street. We hoped to see some sights before our Chinese language and art classes started the next day.

Michael pulled out his map of Taipei and shook it open. "Hey, I hear there's a shopping place down the road called Sogo Department Store. It's like the biggest store here. Why don't we see it?" Michael, tall and thin, had short curly hair and big eyes. Taiwanese girls turned around to gaze at his half-Scottish, half-Chinese features as we passed them.

Karen turned to me. "Jenn, you know how to speak some Chinese. Why don't you ask that lady on the corner how to get to Sogo Department Store?"

Haunted by the three years my mother made me attend Chinese School, I asked the lady: "Where...Sogo...how get there?" The lady looked at me, looked at my friends, laughed and pointed to a bus.

All six of us climbed onto a brown and green bus with no air-conditioning. We dropped 120 NTs into the coin slot as we got in. Karen got in last. I smelled her dewberry perfume. Passengers talked and shoved and pushed into the back of the bus. Their bags reeked of raw fish and greasy duck. The bus driver pointed at Karen and laughed.

"Why did he laugh at you?" asked Michael.

"I don't know." Karen shrugged.

"Look," pointed Tim, "those people are putting money in the box before they get off!"

"I guess over here, you're supposed to pay when you leave the bus," I said.

"Gee, we must've looked like idiots," said Michael.

The Red-Brick Path

The bus honked and manoeuvered around mopeds, bicycles and Honda Civics. Instead of signalling to change lanes, the Taiwanese honked. Steve's long black overcoat swayed back and forth as the bus drove down Gao Shong Main Street. He pulled his bandana back and wiped the sweat off his face.

Tina and Nancy sat in the first empty seats so they could take pictures through the bus window. Locals stared. Karen took out her dewberry-scented talcum powder and rubbed her neck and shoulders to keep her long black hair from sticking to her neck. At every stop, the bus driver stomped on his brakes and we flew forward. Michael and I grasped the greasy metal railing along the ceiling of the bus.

Michael tapped me on the shoulder. "Hey Jenn, I think that's Sogo Department Store." He nodded at a tall pink and grey building.

The bus driver pointed. "Yes, Sogo."

We piled out.

"Thanks man." Tim gave the bus driver a peace sign.

The bus driver nodded and smiled.

Traffic slowed in front of the main entrance to Sogo Department Store. Cars honked and edged over the worn curb, stopping one inch from one another.

"Wow, look at that," Michael pointed.

A large cuckoo clock hung just above the main door of Sogo Department Store. The clock sounded every hour. When it struck three o'clock, a toy blue penguin popped out of a house and pushed a ball that rolled down a slide, around a gate, into a shovel and behind the birdhouse again.

"Sogo must be a Japanese mall," said Karen. "Look at all the cute stuff they have in the window."

Hello Kitty, Kerokerokeroppi and Tuxedo Penguin sat along the edge of the department store window.

"Yeah, I hear Japanese stuff is really popular here," said Tim.

We stood on a red-brick path that resembled the red-brick sidewalks along Queen's Quay West, near Harbourfront in Toronto. On this red-brick path stood a sign. I understood only one character. It meant "no." The second character looked familiar, but I forgot its meaning. The traffic policeman blew his whistle and signalled to the cars that rushed between the underground parking lot and Gao Shong Main Street. He waved his white-gloved hand at us and blew his whistle twice. Michael and I stood in front of Tina, Nancy, Karen and Tim.

"Is he blowing his whistle at us?" Michael whispered.

"I don't think so."

The traffic cop waved his hand again. He spoke to us in Mandarin and blew two short notes.

"Jenn, can you understand what he's saying?" asked Michael.

"No. He said it too fast."

Tina pushed Michael and me aside. "I'm gonna ask him what he's trying to say to us." Her hips swayed as she walked toward the traffic cop. Tina's sandals raised the dust on the red-brick path.

I looked at the sign again. No...no what? What's the second word? Then it hit me. No Pedestrians. The sign read, "No Pedestrians." Before I could yell, a blue Honda Civic accelerated in front of us, swerved onto the red-brick path and bumped Tina's left hip. The mirror on the driver's side fell off and rolled onto the dusty pavement. Tina moved back, looked at the mirror and looked down at her hip.

"Holy shit," said Tim.

The Red-Brick Path

A small woman in a white dress swung the car door open and yelled at Tina in Mandarin. "*Nee yao pay wo...nee yao pay wo....*(You must pay me...You must pay me....)"

Tina's eyes widened.

The woman picked up her mirror and waved it in front of Tina's face. Tina rubbed her left hip. She bit her lip as her eyes welled with tears.

The traffic cop blew his whistle three times, waved his right arm at the woman and Tina and used his left arm to stop the cars from entering the underground parking lot. He came over to Tina. "What were you doing standing on the road?" he asked in Mandarin.

Nancy ran to Tina and spoke to the driver in broken Mandarin. "Tina not understand the red-brick path is road for cars," she said.

The woman spoke quickly to the traffic cop. She waved her arms up and down, crossed and uncrossed them, then reached for a silk handkerchief in her green-flowered purse to wipe sweat from her forehead. The cop touched her shoulder and spoke Mandarin to her. Tina bent down to check her left hip. A small group of locals gathered around Tina, Nancy, the woman and the traffic cop on the red-brick road. Cars waiting to get in and out of the parking lot, honked.

Drivers rolled down their windows and waved their fists. They spat out their windows and lit their cigarettes. The traffic cop held his hand up at them. Shoppers came out of Sogo Department Store to see the commotion. Girls gawked at Michael as they passed our bench. Michael, unaware, brushed back his wavy, brown-black hair with his fingers as the girls giggled.

"What happened?" one shopper asked a man sitting on a bench behind us.

"That lady hit that foreigner," he responded in Mandarin. He pointed at Tina. "I think she's from America."

The woman looked at Tina in disgust. "Ha! Should have just killed her. She's such a big-boned American, no one could have missed her." The woman put her hands on her hips and spat on the ground.

The man leaned back in the bench, laughed, drew back phlegm and spat.

I turned around and saw a familiar face wander out of Sogo Department Store, Counsellor Tom. He had met me and Karen at the Taipei International Airport. I shook Michael and Karen.

"Hey, that's Counsellor Tom!" I said.

Tom came from Toronto too. He had spent his first twelve years in Taiwan, so he spoke both Mandarin and English fluently. We gathered around Counsellor Tom and explained what had happened. Counsellor Tom pushed through the crowd and talked to the traffic cop.

"I think the girl should pay the lady for a new mirror," said the traffic cop.

"No way," Tina said. "I had no idea this was a road. It looks like a sidewalk. Tom, you know what the sidewalks look like in Toronto, you tell him."

Tom spoke to the traffic cop and the traffic cop shook his head. "I warned those kids several times and they wouldn't get off. I even yelled at them between whistles. They just stood there."

"These kids are from Canada. They came here to learn about their parents' culture. You can be a little more understanding."

The traffic cop wrinkled his forehead. "They look Chinese to me. How am I to know that they are foreigners and not smart enough to learn our road laws here?" The traffic cop leaned into

The Red-Brick Path

Counsellor Tom and said in a low voice, "Listen, this is not my responsibility. I don't want to have any part of this. Let's just get the kids to pay off the young lady and we can go back to our business."

I mustered up as much Mandarin as I could remember to make a sentence. "Tina should not pay," I yelled. "That lady was driving too fast."

The woman looked at me and shook her fist.

"Driving fast? Everyone drives at this speed." Then she spoke words I never learned in Chinese school.

Michael called to Counsellor Tom, "Hey, shouldn't they be concerned for Tina? She looks pretty hurt."

Tina's upper lip shook and her cheeks flushed. Nancy put her arm around her. Counsellor Tom told the traffic cop to get a nurse.

"Man, their justice system sucks," Tim said. "If this happened in Canada, the police and ambulance would be here in a second."

The young nurse smiled a lot. She patted Tina's hip and used hand motions to tell Tina to stop touching her bruise.

"Doesn't look too bad." She took first-aid cream from her black bag and gave it to Tina. "It'll heal in a week," she said to Counsellor Tom.

Cars honked and the woman looked around, as if noticing the crowd for the first time. Then she cried. She held her handkerchief tightly against her face. "I've never hit anyone before in my life," she said.

Tina shook and cried. Tears ran down her cheeks and down the side of her neck.

The traffic cop backed away.

Counsellor Tom spoke to Tina, then to the woman. "You've both done some damage to one another and it's no one's fault. Why don't you just shake hands."

Tina took her hand out and shook the woman's hand.

A photographer from the *Taipei Daily News* ran into the crowd and flashed a picture.

Michael turned to me and whispered, "I bet tomorrow's headline will be 'World peace established at last!'"

We laughed.

Tina limped toward us with Counsellor Tom on one side and Nancy on the other. We gathered around Tina, touching her shoulder or her arm. "Are you okay? It wasn't your fault. You gonna be all right?"

Tina nodded. "The bruise isn't all that bad."

The crowd of locals dissipated and the *Taipei Daily News* photographer packed his camera away, pulled his camera bag over his shoulder, lit a cigarette and ran across the street. The traffic cop waved cars in and out of the underground parking lot. Above Sogo Department Store's main doors, the blue penguin popped out of his house and the clock sounded four times. Tina slowly limped into the store with Nancy's left arm wrapped around her waist.

"Careful, take your time," she said. Karen, Tim, Michael, Counsellor Tom and I followed. Karen's dewberry perfume lingered in the moist air. As I flung open the door, Michael turned around.

"I guessed we've learned now to stay off anything that looks like a sidewalk." He laughed, paused, shook his head and walked forward.

Before the door closed behind me, I turned to look at Gao Shong Main Street. Cars zoomed onto the red-brick path and waited to get into the underground parking lot. Dust swirled away from their tires and settled as cars and mopeds honked and revved their engines above the high-pitched shrill of the traffic cop's whistle.

Easter Lilies

In my second year of university, I moved into King's College on the downtown campus of the University of Toronto. I couldn't wait to leave my parents.

That same week Thom died. We'd been buddies since I joined the junior jazz band in high school. My best friend Kim said an undercurrent caught him. My parents assumed he was drunk when he jumped into the icy Humber River. *The Toronto Star* read: "Twenty-two-year-old man drowns in Humber River." Thom was twenty.

At his funeral, the flowers that Kim and I ordered blended in with the other wreaths lined against his coffin. The director of the service asked us to gather by Thom's coffin to say goodbye. I had to look away. Thom must have been under the water for a long time.

"You okay, Jenn?" Kim placed her hand on my shoulder.

"I promised I'd call him before I left for school."

Two days later, Kim left for Guelph and Dad drove me downtown. I'd missed frosh week, house introductions and two days of school. My neighbour, Liz, showed me the pool room, piano room and Dean Sue's office. The rooms all looked the same. I couldn't stop yawning. I had trouble falling asleep. Every time I closed my eyes, I dreamt about Thom's bloated body lying in a large white coffin.

The next day, I followed Liz and her friend Amy to the café. Both in their last year of nursing, Liz and Amy often talked about patient-profile reports and which friend would be engaged next.

"Oh great!" Liz placed a hand on her hip. "Our usual table's full." She looked around the dimly lit cafeteria. "I know, let's go sit with George."

Liz and Amy picked up their trays and headed toward George. I gathered my tray and keys. George sat at the end of the table chewing on a sugar cane as Liz and Amy dropped their trays opposite him. George looked at me as I sat down. I smiled.

"Hi," he said.

"Hi." I poked at my salad as Liz and Amy chatted about what to wear to their friend's wedding.

"My name's George Dickson," he said as he extended a hand to shake mine.

"I'm Jenn."

"So, where are you from, Jenn?"

"Scarborough," I replied. I picked up a chicken leg.

"Oh. That's not very far. I'm from Saskatchewan."

"Really? I never met anyone from Saskatchewan before."

"Yeah, I don't go home very often, but I wanted to study aerodynamic engineering, so I came here."

"Wow, that's a tough field. My brother was in that program."

"Is this your first year living at King's College?"

"Yeah."

"Well, get used to the food. It's only good the first week here."

That evening, I walked back to my room and realized that I hadn't thought about Thom. I called my brother, Steve.

"Hey man! Guess what? I met a guy who's in the same program you were in."

"Oh yeah? Tell him there aren't any jobs for him out there."

"He's from the prairies, y'know!"

"Shit! And he's in engineering science? He must be a genius. You know there's inbreeding going on there, eh?" said Steve.

I laughed. "You're so mean."

In November, our residence paired up with the guys' residence for Movie Night. It was a tradition at King's College. All the girls on my floor went except for Liz and Amy.

"They don't wanna hang with us. They're practically engaged to their boyfriends," said Leanne.

Leanne, also new to King's College, moved in around the same time I did. She lived across from me and we often joked in the hallway until three in the morning, or until Liz or Amy told us to shut up. Leanne and I leaned against the wall and waited for everyone to gather in the front hall to go to the theatre. The door swung open and George walked in.

"Hi," he said.

We talked about what kind of music we like and places we'd like to go to around the world.

After a while, George and I took study breaks together at the Second Cup and went to jazz concerts at Hart House. George came from a town of only five hundred people, smaller than the number of students in my high school graduating class. His town was mainly Cree. He knew how to count to ten in Cree.

When George and I went for coffee, I stopped and looked both ways before I crossed Bloor Street. George sprinted across, even when the way was clear.

"I keep having these nightmares of getting run over in Toronto," he explained. "Rush hour in my town is when two cars actually pass one another on the main road."

George had these innocent-looking brown eyes. Tall and skinny, he always wore a red baseball cap, plaid shirt and jeans. For our residence meal card, he entered a picture of himself in grade two. The lunch lady laughed when she saw his card, so did the rest of the kitchen staff. All the students at King's College knew George. It was always: "Hey George, what's up?" or "George Dickson, late for your math tutorial again?"

When we went to the Thursday-night jazz concerts, he drew me pictures of his Ski-Doo and told me how he would tie a rope to it, put on some skis and have his sister drag him through the snow. His dad owned a small airline company. Their nearest neighbour was at least a mile away. George showed me photos of his dad's planes. A line of small yellow planes with the inscription "Dickson Airlines" stood on ice-covered Kississing Lake. Orange sunsets and blankets of snow filled the background of his photos.

"I love it when it gets below minus forty-five degrees," said George. "The mercury in our thermometer goes berserk. That's when I take one of my dad's planes and drive it around on the ice."

Ever since he was six, when he watched his dad's planes take off over Kississing Lake, George wanted to study aerodynamics.

"I love things that fly," he once told me.

The first of his family to finish high school, George placed in the top ten percent of his engineering class and was one of only three students in his town who went on to university.

"The other two dropped out after first year when they got on probation," he said.

Once I saw George standing on the other side of the café. He looked at me and waved his long arms frantically. I looked the other way because I thought he waved to someone else.

"It's so rude, when people don't say 'hi,'" explained George. "In my town, everyone says 'hi' to each other, even if you don't know them."

On King's College Talent Nights, George played his accordion on stage. Everyone got into it. Some even got up on the stage and danced to the waltzy tunes he played.

One day, as we walked back after a basketball game at SkyDome, George told me how he liked to ride cows on his grandparents' farm and how some people in his town even made clocks out of cow dung.

"You're kidding, right?" I asked.

"No, it's true. We shellac them and hang them on our walls."

I laughed. "Hey is it true that there's inbreeding in the prairies?"

"Who told you that?"

"My brother."

George looked down at the sidewalk. "Actually, come to think of it there's a town thirty miles away from ours and when you look in the phone book, three-quarters of the people there have the last name Cummings...you just gotta wonder."

George and I laughed. As we passed through Union Station, he suddenly stopped and looked up.

"You see those names there?" George pointed at words carved along the top of the walls. "Those are all the stops the train makes in Canada. See that name, Fort Williams? That place is called Thunder Bay now."

"Hey, I never noticed that before," I said.

As we walked along Spadina Crescent, I told George, "I'm definitely going to get a master's degree," and asked, "how 'bout you? You've got the grades to go into med school if you want."

George shook his head.

"Nah, one degree is enough for me. Besides, I wanna get married and have lots of kids after I graduate. A lot of my friends got married right after high school. Two of my best buddies already have kids."

"Wow, that's young," I looked at George. "You know, a friend of mine just died this past September."

"Really? My buddy Ed died last spring. Killed by a drunk driver. The guy got off after three months in jail." George waved his arms in the air. "Totally unfair."

"That's sad," I said. "Some things never end up the way they're supposed to."

"Yeah."

When we reached King's College, we parted at the pathway between the girls' and guys' dormitories.

"Well, Jenn, take'r easy." George waved at me from the steps of the men's residence. I watched him as he ran up the steps, his head bent and his hands in his pocket. As he swung the door open, someone yelled, "Hey George!"

When reading week approached, I decided to stay in residence to work. That's what I told my parents. Then I received a phone call.

"Hey Jenn." It was George. "Wanna come to the Diner with me?" The Diner was a dance club on Gerrard Street, where everyone goes to get hammered.

"Well, I'm working on my essay," I said.

"You know," said George, "a lot of great essays are written under the influence of alcohol."

Before I could say anything, Leanne walked in sipping a Pepsi.

"Hey Leanne."

"What's up?"

"George wants to go to the Diner," I said.

"Okay," said Leanne, "I could use a drink."

When we arrived at the Diner, George bought me and Leanne a rum and Coke. "What do y'know," said George, "my old roomie Jason is here!"

Jason invited us over to his table. Dressed in a plaid shirt and torn jeans, he handed George a beer and introduced us to his girlfriend, Sue.

"Jason and I were roommates last year," said George.

Jason turned his chair around, swung his leg over and planted his large behind on the red cushioned seat.

"I'm in charge of cleaning and maintenance on our floor," said Jason. He smelled like beer. "Y'know the cleaning lady uses the same brush to clean the toilets and the sink?"

"That's nasty." Sue wrinkled up her nose.

"Man, I drop my toothbrush in the sink all the time," I said.

"You might as well drop it in a toilet," said George.

I laughed. Jason squinted his eyes at me.

"Are you Chinese?"

"Yeah," I said, "but I was born in Canada."

Leanne gave me a half-smile.

Jason turned to George. "I tried to study today, but the karaoke was just blastin' in the hallway."

George laughed. "White people are a minority in Toronto."

"Tell me about it," said Leanne.

I looked at her in shock.

"I'm from Blind River and I just couldn't get used to it in my first year here. Toronto makes me nervous."

"Yeah," said Jason, "everyone from my town is European or of European descent."

"Where are you from, Jason?" I asked.

"Thunder Bay. You hardly see Chinese people there. In fact, the only Chinese person in my town owns a laundromat!"

"Oh yeah?" added Leanne. "The Chinese guy in my town owns the laundromat and restaurant."

Jason laughed and handed Sue another beer. I sipped my beer quietly. I leaned against my chair and watched Jason, George, Leanne and Sue laugh together. After a minute, I caught George staring at me. I stared back and smiled. He turned away.

Over dinner, for the next two weeks, Leanne wouldn't stop talking about George. "Isn't he nice? He bought us both a drink and he's so cute! That's what I need, Jenn, a nice, small-town boy. You don't really like him, do you? Besides, you guys aren't of the same stock. My mom always told me to stay within your kind, y'know? I don't think George has any strong feelings for you either."

Leanne licked her thick, chocolate-butterscotch ice-cream and wrapped her dyed blond hair around her finger. "Hi George," she yelled as he passed our table.

George didn't hear her.

"Oh, hey Jenn!" He plopped his tray down and waved with his long arm in the air.

"Hey," I said.

I didn't talk to Leanne for a while. I told her I preferred studying on my own, and went to bed earlier than usual.

"Serious problem," wrote Kim in her e-mail message. "Don't go for small-town guys, Jenn. Next thing you know, you'll have a bunch of half-breed kids on a dairy farm."

"Oh, he might be a nice guy," said Steve over the phone.

"What do you mean?" I was surprised he'd make such a kindhearted comment.

"You just gotta look under the white hood Jenn." Steve burst out laughing.

As exam time approached, I concentrated on getting my essays done so I would have more time to study. George sent me a large package the day after the Easter Weekend—beautiful white Easter lilies.

"It's just a friendly thing," I explained to Leanne.

"No, Jenn, you don't send friends flowers unless they're sick or something," said Leanne.

I tried to forget what she said.

The day before exam week, the phone rang at two in the morning.

"Jenn? Did I wake you?" asked George.

"Kinda, I was just getting ready for bed," I said. "By the way, thanks for the Easter lilies."

"I'm glad you like them. You know, there's a story behind Easter lilies. My grandmother gave Easter lilies to a friend four years ago. When my grandmother died last year, my dad called her friend up to tell her. The friend wasn't even surprised when she found out. She said she kind of figured it out because after four years, the Easter lilies never bloomed. She would water them and everything. Then one day they did bloom. They bloomed on the same day my grandmother died. Isn't that funny?"

"That's pretty neat. Are they still alive now?"

"Yeah, the friend planted them in her garden." George was quiet for a while. "Listen...Jenn, I called for a reason. I...I have this problem. I think you're the nicest girl I've ever met and I was wondering if…we could be more than friends."

"No…no, I can't. I don't know why, I just can't George," I blurted out, half-awake. We were quiet for a while, then I thought I heard him cry.

"Are you okay?"

"No," George sniffled.

"Maybe we should talk about this tomorrow."

"But…but what if the world ends tomorrow?" George spoke between sobs.

I imagined him sitting by his desk, clutching the phone as tears filled his big brown eyes and streamed down his cheeks.

"Jenn, I have to go work in Calgary for four months after exams end and I won't even be able to see my family."

"Well, why don't you cancel the job in Calgary and find a job in Saskatchewan?" I said.

"I don't want to. This is the first time I got a job with an engineering company," George sniffled. "Why is life so complicated, Jenn? Everything seems to be ending and I wish I could take all my friends and put them in a truck and drive them wherever I go."

"I don't think we can all fit in the truck," I said.

I couldn't go back to sleep that night. I couldn't work on an essay due in two days. I spent the entire weekend worrying over George.

"You made him cry? What the hell did you do that for?" screamed Liz when I told her in the bathroom.

"Beats me. I mean it wasn't like we were going out or anything. We just hung around each other."

"Look what you've done. You've corrupted an innocent prairie boy. He's never gonna speak to you again!"

"I don't think it's just me, though. I think he probably left home too early. I mean, how would you feel going to a place that's totally different from what you're used to?" My nose ran. I had been sneezing all day. "I think I'm allergic to these lilies."

"What are you gonna do?"

I gave Liz a big grin. "I have an idea."

It rained that night. Small drops trickled down my nose and onto my windbreaker. I wrapped the Easter lilies carefully in a bag and took out the small silver shovel I had bought at White Rose after dinner. We went to the garden by the Earth Sciences Building.

"This place is good," I said.

"Jenn, it's a sample of the Canadian Boreal Forest."

"I know, but the soil looks stable." We planted the lilies between two white pines. As I patted the soil with my small shovel, I thought about how much I'd miss George.

"Every time I think of Saskatchewan and Ski-Doos and oncoming traffic I'll think of you," I said to the lilies.

As we left, Liz made joking sniffle sounds.

"You know what's going to happen Jenn?" asked Liz as we headed back. "Maintenance will find them and dig them up in less than a week. Either that, or the lilies will multiply and next thing you know it, you've ruined the whole ecosystem."

When I returned to my room, the phone rang. It was George.

"Guess what? I aced my exam! It was so easy. I thought I'd fail it."

Great. I know I failed my essay, I thought.

"Listen, I'm sorry for the way I acted over the weekend. I'll still go to jazz concerts and on coffee runs with you. You'll always be my friend, Jenn. I don't know what was wrong with me that night. It's just that," George sighed, "life can be so complicated at times."

"Well, I hope you have a good time in Calgary. I know I'd love to see that place if I had the chance."

"My dad flies there all the time, nothing special there. I'm...I'm really going to miss Toronto, Jenn."

"I know."

I gave George my address.

He never wrote.

I wondered what would have happened if I had gone out with George. I imagined holding his hand and being dragged through oncoming traffic. I missed George and his funny stories.

Later that summer, I brought Kim to the Earth Sciences garden. It had been almost a year since Thom died and I had fewer and fewer dreams about him now.

"Jenn, my feet are tired. I don't see why we're walking through here," said Kim.

We stopped near the Easter lilies. The flowers had wilted and fallen, but the stem stood strong against the heavy wind. Kim and I knelt down by the lilies. I turned to Kim.

"You know," I said, "there's a story behind these lilies.... "

Derrick

Derrick Tsang, large and tall, wore a black fur jacket and a furry black cap with flaps that hung down the side of his face. I walked behind him on the way home from Woodcrest Public School. My older brother, Steven, wouldn't walk home with me because it embarrassed him to be seen with his six-year-old sister, so I followed Derrick. Derrick walked slower than Steve. I could catch up to Derrick.

Derrick lived two doors down from our house on Avongate Road, only a block away from Woodcrest Public School, but the walk seemed a mile long.

When I ran in the snow, my mittens dangled beside me from a string that attached them to my purple snow coat.

"Hey Jenn," Derrick said, "can you run to the end of the driveway? I think you're a really fast runner. Can you do that?"

I nodded and sprinted as fast as I could across Mrs. Rosen's driveway, my boots pushing the powdery snow behind me. I fell into the snow, face first. Snow covered my eyelashes, nose and mouth. Derrick had tripped me. I tried to get up. My boots slipped and slid on the wet driveway.

Derrick laughed.

"Sorry Jenn. I'm so sorry." He wiped snow off my jacket. "Here." He handed me a Kleenex.

I didn't cry. I smiled instead. This happened often. Derrick would ask me to run for him, then trip me and apologize.

Eventually, I didn't want to go to school, so I told Mom about Derrick.

"You just tell him to stop," said Mom. "Just yell out 'No' in a big voice. Say, 'I don't like that.' Okay?"

The next time I saw Derrick in front of me, I slowed down. Derrick turned around. I backed up.

"I don't want you tripping me anymore," I said.

"Okay. I won't. But can you run again? I wanna see how fast you can go."

I did.

He tripped me.

I got up and wiped snow off my face.

Derrick grinned. "I didn't say I promised!"

Derrick held my shoulders and asked me to yell as loud as I could.

I said no.

He took his snow-covered glove and slapped me on the face.

I yelled.

"Louder," he said.

"Ahhhh," I yelled.

"That doesn't sound like a yell."

"Ahhhh," I yelled louder.

Derrick tripped me and pushed snow into my mouth.

I tried to get up, but he stepped on my mittens and snapped the string.

Derrick

I told Mom. Mom walked over to see Derrick's parents but found no one home. I told her to forget about it. Maybe I would too. I had met a new friend, Marie. Marie and I walked home together every day. Derrick never touched Marie. She had three older brothers. She was white.

Mom talked to Mrs. Smith, the grade six teacher at Woodcrest Public School. Mom knew Mrs. Smith because Mom volunteered at the school library and helped organize Chinese New Year.

A week later, I saw Derrick again.

"You told your mom, didn't you?" He squinted at me.

I smiled.

Derrick turned and walked down Avongate Road alone.

I didn't see Derrick for a long time. I thought the Tsang family had moved. My parents had never really talked with the Tsangs except to say "Hi" or "How are things?"

Dad described the Tsangs as a different kind of family than us. They came from Trinidad and they owned a restaurant. "They are working class."

"But you work, too," I said.

"That's different," Dad mumbled and turned the ruffled pages of *The Globe and Mail*.

Dad worked as a senior engineer for Ontario Hydro. Sometimes he spoke as a guest lecturer at York or the University of Toronto.

"Dad and I came here on university scholarships," Mom explained. "We are not like the earlier Chinese immigrants who came here to open restaurants and convenience stores. Our family...well, we have different values."

One summer after I turned twenty-two, I saw Derrick as I biked home after work. Derrick rounded the corner of Avongate Road. He hunched beneath the weight of a backpack that hung off his right shoulder. I recognized him when he looked up. I smiled.

He nodded.

"Are you Derrick?" I asked.

"Yeah."

"I thought you and your family moved."

"Nah. We're still around. My sister and I just work the night shift, that's all." Derrick bent to tie his shoelaces. His hairline had receded.

"Wow. You've sure grown." He looked me up and down. "Been away at university?"

"Uh-huh. U of T. Where did you go?"

"I didn't. Couldn't take high school anymore. Went to Humber College instead." Derrick looked down at the cracked pavement of Mrs. Rosen's driveway.

"Oh yeah? What did you study?"

"Graphics. Computer graphics."

"That sounds interesting."

"Nah. I took it four years ago. Now they got this new program that's replacing all of us and I spent so long in school just to get this degree." Sweat slid down the side of Derrick's face. He wiped it away. "My degree was so useless and this night shift shit is getting me real tired. I was thinking of moving out."

"It's fun living away," I said.

"Oh yeah? You've done it?"

"I live downtown during the year."

"What are you studying?"

"English."

"English? Wow. That's a course I could never pass. Hated high school. Hey, how old is Steve now?"

Derrick

"He's twenty-nine."

"He married?" asked Derrick.

"No."

"Twenty-nine and not married? Man, I'm twenty-seven and my parents are, like, hounding me. It's just so hard to meet people when you work the night shift all the time." Derrick talked about movies and how hard it was to find a good job. He talked as if he hadn't talked to anyone in a long time. I circled Mrs. Rosen's cracked pavement with my ten-speed. Derrick took off his glasses and wiped the sweat away.

"How old are you now, Jenn?"

"I'm twenty-two."

"Oh. That's still young. I'd give anything to be in your shoes."

I got off my bike as we got closer to my house. I felt two feet taller than Derrick. Derrick looked at me. "I guess I better mosey on down now," he said. Halfway down the sidewalk, Derrick paused and turned around. "Boy. You've grown." He looked me up and down again. "Well, say hi to Steve and your parents for me, 'kay?"

"Okay."

Before I opened the garage to put my ten-speed back inside, I turned to look at Derrick. I wanted to ask him if he remembered all the times he tripped me in the snow when I was six years old.

Derrick crossed the street. His bag pulled down on his right shoulder. I watched him as he walked, slightly hunched, pushing the gravel with his worn leather shoes.

I locked my bike up and closed the garage.

Chinese Christmas

"You kids have no culture!" Auntie Fong waves her chopsticks at Christopher, Daniel, Steven and me.

Once again, our family spends Christmas night at Golden Dragon Restaurant. Auntie Fong and Auntie Yan sit across from us at the kids' table. Sick with the flu, they sit far away from the adults. Uncle Wong arrives late and sits at the kids' table with us. Steven is twenty-seven and I am twenty-one and we still have to sit at the kids' table.

The last time we spent Christmas at Golden Dragon Restaurant, Mom went to New York to take care of her father, Wai-gon, who caught the flu. Dad didn't want to cook, so he took me, Steven, his parents, *A-gon* and *Nai-nai*, out for dinner.

"What's the matter, Nai-nai?" Dad asks his mom as we sit down to order. Nai-nai wriggles her small hands up the wide sleeves of her *qi pao* (traditional Chinese dress) and clicks her plastic dentures together.

"Nothing," she squeaks in her mouse-tiny voice.

Nai-nai twists her size-five feet so her toes point inwards. She wears the same sized shoes I wore when I was seven years old. Mom once told me she used to have her feet bound until she turned nine. All women from aristocratic families had their feet bound.

"Must've hurt," I thought.

Nai-nai clicks her dentures again.

"C'mon, Nai-nai something must be wrong," urges Dad.

Nai-nai shivers and shifts in her chair.

"Han!" A-gon calls her by her Chinese name. "What's the matter?"

"I think Nai-nai is cold," I say.

"No, I'm fine," says Nai-nai quietly. She folds her arms over her chest.

I look up and point to the ceiling. "It's the fan above us. It's making her cold."

Dad waves his hand at a waiter. "Can we move to another table? The fan above us will give my mother a cold."

The waiter looks up at the fan, then looks at us. He and Dad walk over to the next table. Dad holds his hands out and looks up again. The waiter looks up. Dad shakes his head. My stomach growls, then Steven's. Dad walks to a corner table and says something in Cantonese to the waiter. The waiter looks up and waves his hand to call us over. I hold Nai-nai's hand and guide her over to the corner table.

When we finally settle down, Dad tells Steven to switch chairs with Nai-nai. "Better put her in the corner, just in case," says Dad.

Dad moves our coats, then Nai-nai's purse. We shuffle around.

Dad orders in Cantonese and points at the menu as he speaks to the waiter.

"Look, Jenn." Steven points to the rest of the people in the restaurant.

Everyone in the restaurant stares at the ceiling, looking confused.

We have no turkeys or Christmas trees or extravagant gift exchanges on Christmas day. We are usually one of four families in the Chinese restaurant. I wonder what the other families do.

Chinese Christmas

Instead of turkey, we have pig. Uncle Wong serves me three spoonfuls of pig. I like the skin the best. If you say you don't want any more, the waiter will put more on your plate. It's a custom. Only Chinese people do this. Once my friend Kim Johnson came over for dinner on my sixteenth birthday, and Mom spent all day making wonton soup and Cantonese chicken with noodles. Kim didn't want any. She shook her head and wrinkled up her nose when Mom came to her seat at the table. Mom wanted to fatten Kim up, make her nice and healthy, so she took her wooden chopsticks and plopped an extra large serving on Kim's plate. Kim almost threw up trying to finish the noodles. The year after, Kim left before dinner. Mom suggested we order pizza instead.

I reach for some more pig with my chopsticks. Auntie Fong stares at me longer than usual, then sighs.

"I worry about my Joanne," says Auntie Fong. "She eighteen now and does not like Chinese boys. I say, 'Hey, that boy in your class, Charlie Wong, he good-looking,' but she just make a face. *Ai-yaa*, you young kids, different taste, eh?"

Steven and I look at each other. Auntie Fong looks at Auntie Yan.

"Joanne like this boy now. White boy." Auntie Fong reaches for a slice of pig and dips it in the sweet and sour sauce. "She think he good-looking. I see him. Sooo ugly." Auntie Fong wrinkles up her face and presses her cheeks with her index finger. "Too much, how you say, too much...freckle. *Ai-yo*."

Uncle Wang clicks his ivory chopsticks together and reaches for some pig. He plops the fatty slice on his plate and points his chopsticks at Auntie Fong.

"My Debbie...she brought home a Jewish boy for dinner last night. So funny. He's a Russian Jew! Never heard of that."

"What will happen to our next generation? Get mixed blood in the family, that's what!" Auntie Fong chews on a slice of pig leg, then throws it on the waste plate and looks at Daniel, Christopher, Steven and me. "You kids like my Joanne, only prefer *yaan-ren?*"

I stare at Steven and laugh.

"Well, I guess it would depend on what the person is really like, you know, their personality," says Steven.

I nod.

Auntie Fong presses her lips together.

"Not me," says Daniel. "I can't go with a Chinese chick. Those Hong Kong immigrants in my high school are always talking on the 'cellophane.' Man, I can't stand that!" Daniel leans back in his chair and reaches for an icy mug of Molson Canadian beer.

"I'm so afraid my Debbie will marry the Russian Jew," says Uncle Wong. He shakes his head. "She brought him home for Christmas. Must mean something serious."

Auntie Fong picks up a greasy chopstick and squints. "Now, which one of you," she says, pointing the soy-sauce stained ends of her ivory chopstick at us, "Which one of you will marry a *yaan-ren?*"

I slide lower in my seat and Steven looks away.

Auntie Lam looks down. Her son, Walter, married an English girl and her daughter, Nancy, married an Italian. Dad, the MC for their reception, had to speak Italian and Chinese that night. He was so nervous on stage we couldn't tell when he spoke Italian and when he spoke Chinese.

"Rei-we," Auntie Yan points her chopsticks at Daniel, "Rei-we is going out with a white girl now."

"Hang your head in shame, Daniel," I say.

Christopher and I laugh.

The clock beside the karaoke machine reads eleven o'clock. We have to leave soon, but the pig is only half eaten. I pick out the less fatty parts. I hate chewing fat. Steven likes it, so I put the fatty parts on his plate.

Auntie Fong smiles at me. "Have some more pig Wei-Shin," she says, calling me by my Chinese name, she plops the fattest strips onto my plate. "You young kids must stay healthy. You represent the new generation."

Steven, Christopher, Daniel and I finish the strips of pig while Auntie Fong and Auntie Yan sing a Chinese love song with the karaoke machine.

The clock reads twelve. I feel stuffed. We gather at the main doors of Golden Dragon Restaurant and wait for Steven to pull up his new Ford Probe. He washes it every night and never lets me drive it. He parks it in a special spot in our driveway and checks its position the next day to see if it has been moved, afraid that I take it out for joy-rides. I only did that once and forgot to release the emergency brake so the Probe went really slow.

Steven pulls the car up front of the Golden Dragon Restaurant and I help Nai-nai into the back seat. Auntie Fong hugs Steven and me tightly.

"I bring Joanne over to U of T to see you someday," she whispers in my ear.

"Okay," I say.

As I close the door, snow falls, big chunks of snow.

"*Mei*," Nai-nai taps me on the shoulder. "Can you tighten my seat belt?"

I tighten the straps around her small body. Her hair has turned ivory white since she stopped dying it. When the car stops at an intersection, I tap Dad's shoulder.

"Dad, would you get mad if I didn't marry a Chinese guy?" I whisper.

"No. Up to you." Dad motions to Steven to tell him to turn on the windshield wipers. "If nice, from good family, then it okay." Dad turns back to face the front window, pauses and turns to me again. "Just remember, if you bring any guy home, I going to knock him out first, take blood sample and test to see if he got AIDS. If all right, then you can see him." Dad turns to face the front again.

When the green light flashes, Steven steps on the gas pedal. I sit back, lean against Nai-nai and think of all the pig I ate.

Beijing Heat

The temperature has hit forty-four degrees Celsius in Beijing. Val and I walk down Sun Li Tun Street, the Foreign Fashion District of Beijing. I plan to buy a North Face fleece jacket, and Val, some Gucci wallets and Armani shoes. Most brand name products are cheap because they are either stolen or slightly defective. T-shirts, fleece tops and jeans hang from fences that separate one vendor from another. Elderly women sit outside their stores fanning themselves with bamboo fans. "Hello friend," they yell as we pass them with our empty backpacks, ready to load with new clothes. Val has a Montreal flag sewn on the back of hers. I like to go shopping with Val because she bargains well.

"Eighty *quei*," says the saleswoman when Val holds up a Polo fleece jacket.

Val puts up four fingers, "Forty *quei*," she says in broken Chinese.

Born in Wenzhou, China, Val moved with her family to Spain when she was four and lived there until she was nine. They moved to Toronto, then to Montreal, where they opened a Chinese restaurant. Now they own two Chinese restaurants and a Japanese restaurant.

Val speaks two dialects in Chinese, Putonghua and Wenzhouhua, as well as Spanish, French and English.

"No, friend," says the woman, "sixty quei."

Val shakes her head. "Twenty."

"Okay, I give you forty."

"Twenty."

"Thirty-five."

"Twenty."

"Twenty-five." Val takes my arm and we walk away.

The woman looks at us, purses her lips and waves at us.

"Eh, *hue lai*...come back. I give you for twenty."

Val grins at me, takes the Polo fleece and hands a hundred dollar bill to the lady. The woman swears at Val, licks her teeth and counts the change.

"Come on. Give me thirty-five for it. Okay?" she asks in Chinese. "*Ni shi hua-ren*, overseas Chinese, right?"

We nod.

"You must have lots of money. Help a friend, okay?" The woman puts her hands out like she is begging. I notice her thick skin and spots of brown on her cheek. She has high cheek bones, a typical northern Chinese feature.

I look at her and the cardboard sheet behind her where a two-year-old girl curls up for her afternoon nap. A red plastic sandal hangs off her right foot. I would have given her the full price if she asked for it, but Val shakes her head and says in a stern voice. "*Ga wo qian.* (Hand the change over.)"

Val holds her palm out.

The woman stares at Val's long nails painted in red and glittery gold. She licks her teeth again and hands over the full change.

"That poor lady," I say to Val.

"Nah, she's just lying. She's probably stinking rich. The Chinese cheat each other." Val brushes her long hair back over her shoulders. She dyes her hair blond and rubs blue eyeshadow on her upper eyelids so they look like she has deepset eyes. The youngest of her two sisters and brother, she is the first girl in her family who refuses to have an arranged marriage.

"I don't want to get married," Val says to me.

"Why?" I ask.

"Because my parents only believe in arranged marriages. In our family, we have to marry Chinese and both my sisters had disaster marriages because they had arranged marriages with Chinese men from Wenzhou. One beats my oldest sister and the other one will not stop smoking and blows my sister's money gambling at casinos." Val looks at me and says angrily, "Both my sisters work very hard and they have PhDs in chemistry and electrical engineering. These bastards don't even have anything close to a college degree."

"Didn't anyone check their background before they came to Canada?"

"No, I think they just wanted to get an easy ticket out of China. Both men are real good looking…for Chinese," says Val.

"So? If your parents wanted them to marry Chinese, they could have married a Chinese guy from Canada. Why look in China? I mean it's so different. What would your sisters have in common with them?"

"Well, take a good look at me."

I look at Val. Despite her dyed hair, she looks like the women we pass in Beijing. She has a flat nose and slanted eyes. The corners of her mouth point downwards.

"I'm not exactly pretty, you know. My sisters look like me." Val looks down at the road. "My sisters knew they wouldn't find a guy without an arranged marriage so they at least wanted a good-looking guy. I mean, everyone wants to go to Canada, so they get something too...."

"Hmmm...Your family's very traditional," I say.

"Yeah, tell me about it."

I take out a tissue to wipe the sweat that rolls down my neck and my chin.

"Want one?" I ask.

Val takes a tissue and reaches down her shirt to wipe her chest.

"It's so hot I could just die."

We pass a McDonald's. A plump little boy runs out with an ice cream in one hand and fries in the other. His grandmother follows after him.

"Little Emperor," says Val.

The air conditioning blows against our faces.

"Ahhhh," I lean my head back, "Let's go in."

Inside McDonald's, every table is filled. Two high-school girls sit and chat. At the same table, a boy and girl sit together holding hands and sharing Chicken McNuggets. Only half of the people buy food. In Beijing, one McDonald's meal costs the same as a meal at a fancy restaurant in Canada.

"Where can we sit?"

"Gee, I don't know," I say. I look at a table to my right. A Chinese man in his fifties chews on a McChicken. Two empty seats face him. "You don't think he would let us sit across from him, do you?" I look around. Everywhere strangers sit with strangers.

"Why don't you ask him?" Val nudges me.

"Why don't you?"

"Your Chinese is better."

"Yeah, well you should be practicing yours."

Val looks around. "Listen, if we can't get a place, we can eat outside on the bench."

"It's too hot. I'm not eating outside," I say as I shift my feet.

"Fine, then you ask him."

"But it's so weird sitting in front of someone we don't know. I mean, we can't exactly have a conversation with him," I say.

"But if he doesn't understand me then we might lose a place." I stare at Val. "What do you want me to do?"

She stares impatiently back at me. We both stare at the Chinese man as he chews his McChicken. Val taps her feet.

I fling my arms in the air. "Fine."

Facing the Chinese man, I take a deep breath and say, "*Qing wen, you ren ma?*"

The man looks up at us, then waves his hand at the empty seats and nods.

"See, wasn't that easy?" says Val.

We drop our bags and lean back in our chairs. I order a Coke and Chicken Nuggets. Val orders an ice cream sundae and fries.

"Look at that." I point to a poster of the Beatles. "That's old, eh? I didn't know the Beatles are still popular here." I chew on one of Val's fries.

The Chinese man sits motionless across from us. He chews slowly on his McChicken.

"Can you name them all?"

"Well, the one on the right is Paul McCartney, the one sitting down is John Lennon...." I look at the man.

He stares blankly ahead and chews.

"The one on the left is Ringo Starr...Hmmm...who's the other one sitting down?"

"I don't know. I don't think he ever did anything after the Beatles."

"I don't think so either," says Val. "I used to know his name, though. It's on the tip of my tongue...."

We shuffle our feet. I reach for more fries.

"George Harrison," says the man in perfect, fluent English. "The picture was taken in '71." The man wrinkles his nose. "But that's before your time."

Val and I look at each other. We look at the man.

The man turns back and chews his McChicken.

Copenhagen Mermaid

The Copenhagen Mermaid sits on a single rock near the Langeline Harbour, overlooking Malmö, Sweden. Her left arm rests on the softly carved scales of her lap. Her right arm presses lightly against a carved black rock. Her head is turned slightly, as if gazing over the harbour, and her back bends slightly, leaning towards the water. Her braided hair drapes down her curved back.

I flew to Copenhagen to see Corrina, a friend I met while studying in Beijing.

"I am sorry I cannot spend all my time with you. My boss will not give me extra time off because we have a colleague on vacation," says Corrina.

"It's okay," I say. "I think I'll join a walking tour during the daytime anyway."

Corrina brushes back her straight black hair and puts on her sunglasses. She pulls her boyfriend towards her.

"This is Andy," she says.

"Nice to meet you." Andy shakes my hand and reaches for my suitcase and places it in the trunk of the Mercedes Benz taxi.

"We ordered a Mercedes Benz just for you," says Andy.

Corrina laughs and slaps him on the arm. "All our taxis in Copenhagen are Mercedes Benz. It is better for the air."

Corrina's house looks like my house in Mississauga. There are three floors, a garage and a small backyard. Red roses line the front porch, like mine. Inside, there are catalinas and spider plants hanging by the windowsill.

"You have the same plants my parents have."

"Probably because Chinese families think alike no matter where they are," says Andy as he places my suitcase by the door. "I need to go study now, but call me if you go missing. I am more free in the day than Corrina." He hands me his cell phone number.

Corrina's father and mother walk into the kitchen. Her mom places a bag of rice on the floor by the kitchen sink. Corrina slaps Andy on the arm. "Say goodbye to my parents, eh?"

"*Zai-jian,*" says Andy. Corrina's mother smiles at him.

I bow my head a little and greet Mr. and Mrs. Chan in Mandarin. We shake hands.

"Sit, sit," says Mrs. Chan in Cantonese, motioning to me. I understand some words. She gestures for Corrina to bring in a chair. Mrs. Chan, small in stature with big round eyes, looks like an older version of Corrina. She pours orange juice into a glass cup and places it in front of me.

"Mango pudding?" asks Mr. Chan and mumbles something to me.

Corrina slaps her father on the arm.

"Jennifer doesn't speak Danish, silly, she's from Canada."

"Oh, oh," Mr. Chan speaks loudly and brushes his thick black hair behind his ears. "I say, feel like at home," he pauses and sits down.

We laugh. I gulp down the orange-coloured pudding.

"The lady who bought my parents' restaurant taught my mom how to make this," says Corrina.

Mrs. Chan nods politely at me.

I smile.

"We just sell our restaurant six months ago, but must start again soon. We are running out of money." Mrs. Chan shakes her head. "I don't want to start again," she says in Mandarin. "It's so hard working ten hours a day. Ai-yo, I get so tired and the oil sizzles in my face all the time. But this is how life is." She smiles and spoons more mango pudding onto my plate.

Mrs. Chan pulls a chair back and sits in front of me.

Corrina suddenly stands up and runs to her room.

"Don't come in yet!" she yells. "My room is still very messy!"

Mr. Chan clears his throat, looks me up and down.

"So, what your parents do in Canada? They own Chinese restaurant or store?"

I gulp down the pudding. "My dad is an engineer," I say. "My mom stays at home."

Mr. Chan nods. "Oh. All overseas Chinese always has to work hard to make a living. It's not easy anywhere." He looks at Mrs. Chan.

Mrs. Chan smiles at me.

"No, this is not how you do it," says Mr. Chan in Cantonese.

I sit in Peking Ancient Chinese Restaurant in Tivoli Square, the heart of Copenhagen, with Corrina and Mr. Chan's friends.

"I made appointments to meet my friends for dinner a long time ago, so you can also come along," said Mr. Chan. "They are all famous restaurant owners, one from Copenhagen and another visiting from Hong Kong. My good friends."

"At my restaurant we place the forks here and the serviettes like this," says Mr. Fong.

"No, no," says Mr. Lai. He waves his large hands and pushes back his thick black glasses. "We do like this." He speaks in English for me and looks me in the eye. Mr. Lai folds the serviette in two and creases the centre with his right index finger.

"Mr. Lai started out as a dishwasher and now he owns one of the most famous restaurants in Hong Kong," whispers Corrina. "They only serve government executives, so he knows how to prepare serviettes real well."

Mr. Chan and Mr. Fong watch Mr. Lai. Mr. Lai folds the serviette again. As his index finger creases the centre, I notice his yellowed, brittle nail, his thick finger pads and the dry cracks along the sides of his fingers. Mr. Lai licks his finger and folds again and again, then, quickly and neatly pulls on a corner and three folded ends unravel. On the palm of his right hand sits a serviette peacock.

Mr. Fong smiles and claps.

Mr. Lai smiles.

The restaurant manager, an older lady dressed in a green suit and skirt, rests her arm on Mr. Chan's shoulder. "How is everything?"

"Very well. Excellent business you are having tonight." Mr. Chan gives her a thumbs up.

The manager collects our plates and places a dish of eggplant and shrimp in front of us.

"Your restaurants are so nice here," I say to Corrina. "It seems like all your Chinese restaurants here are very fancy and you even have menus only in English."

"If we do not meet government standards then we have to close down," says Corrina. "They have very high standards here."

I smile at the Danish waitress dressed in a Chinese *chi-pao* as she places a plate of sizzling Chinese mushrooms and thin bamboo strips with oyster sauce in front of me. As she walks away, her blonde ponytail bounces up and down and brushes the collar of her *chi-pao*.

As we eat, Danish customers stare at us.

"Why are they looking?" I whisper to Corrina.

"Because they don't usually serve these meals at this restaurant. It is because Mr. Lai is here that they make special plates."

"What do they usually serve?" I ask.

"Look around," says Corrina.

At the table beside us, a Danish lady slurps spaghetti using chopsticks. Her husband munches on fish and chips.

"Every Chinese restaurant has this," whispers Corrina. "It is in case the visitors don't like fried rice or Chinese soup. They serve spaghetti and fish and chips and steak with lots of ketchup." Corrina wrinkles her nose.

During the day, I buy a Copenhagen Card that lets me ride the bus to museums and tourist sites. Mr. Chan drives me to the Radhousplatzen, Copenhagen's city centre, where I can walk to the Museum of Design or the New Carlsberg Museum.

"When it rains," explains the tour guide, "they wheel out the statue of a golden lady on a bike, holding a parasol. She sits just below the clock tower. When it is going to be sunny, the lady without the parasol comes out."

Andy rides up on his tenspeed bicycle.

"Beep, beep!" he says. "How you enjoying everything?" he asks.

Andy is Vietnamese and arrived in Copenhagen as a refugee eight years ago. He speaks Danish with an accent. We walk down Vinderbrogade, a wide street lined with museums. Andy points to every statue and design and explains its Viking history.

"How do you know all this?" I ask.

"Oh, I read a lot. I read and read when I came to this country. The one thing I like about Copenhagen is if you tell them you are a student, they let you into museums for free. They really encourage education here. Almost everyone has a university degree and more and more are getting master's degrees. We have one of the highest educated populations in the world."

Andy buys me a chocolate-covered waffle from the city square. The warm waffle melts in my mouth. Chocolate drips onto my fingers and I lick it off.

Andy laughs.

"Good, yah?" I peel off a piece for him. "When you were in Berlin did you go to any clubs?" he asks.

"No."

"Well, we will take you to one tonight. We are meeting some friends just outside of Copenhagen."

Fong bounces her baby on her lap. We could hear the ten-month-old's screams from the hall before we entered the apartment. Andy makes faces at Fong's baby.

"When you arrive, Jennifer?" smiles Fong.

"Two days ago. I leave tomorrow."

"Too bad you can't stay longer," says Fong's brother, Vinni. Vinni, tall and well built, with brown and black hair, was born in Denmark, right after the family came from Vietnam. Different from his timid sister and soft-spoken brother, Vinni sits confidently, legs apart. He gestures like all the other Danes using his hands a lot when he talks and speaks fluent Danish. He recently finished high school. Since his mother's fourth kidney operation last year, he works at the family Chinese take-out restaurant in Copenhagen's city centre.

Vinni's mother chops radishes in the kitchen. She pokes her head through the doorway. "You speak good English," she says in Mandarin. "Your parents also own a restaurant in Canada?"

"No." I smile and walk into the kitchen.

Vinni's mother winces and touches her lower back. "My back hurts all the time from walking, but my boys and my daughter are so helpful here. I have another daughter in San Francisco, America. She is a successful accountant. She has two kids now."

"Jennifer." Vinni grabs my hand. "Let me show you around the apartment." We walk down the narrow hallway. On the bare wall a large crack runs down the left side from the left corner, slowly growing thinner as it gets to the doorway. Vinni opens a door.

"Here is water closet," he says. "Don't mind my sister's stockings." I laugh. The bathtub is smaller than the one I have at home. The taps are silver and rusting. Tube socks and stockings hang from the shower bar. Vinni pulls my arm again.

"Here my room." He steps proudly inside. "I share with my brother but now he work nightshift so I have all to myself." Vinni stretches his arms out. A box of CDs sits on the floor betweem two bunkbeds. A string stretches from the window to the door. Laundry clips hang from the string and a laundry basket sits near the closet.

"You want to stay here tonight?" he whispers in my right ear.

I edge away from him and smile. "That's okay," I laugh.

Vinni looks at me and I feel my cheeks grow warm.

"Okay, okay," he laughs.

Vinni hands me a Carlsberg beer and we sit down in their living room, which connects to the kitchen.

"Welcome to Denmark…*Skhole*." He clinks his beer can against mine. "That is 'cheers' in Danish."

"Oh, *Skhole*," I say.

"So, you can speak English, Mandarin and French?" asks Vinni.

"No," says his brother, Duong, "they don't all have to learn French there."

"Yes, they do."

"No, they don't."

The two argue in a mix of Cantonese and Danish.

I smile at the sing-song tune of the two languages, the long *u* sounds from the back of the throat and the soft consonants.

"How come you don't like to speak Chinese?" asks Andy.

"I prefer English because it's easier."

"But you learned Chinese with Corrina in Beijing last year."

"Yeah, but I'm not very good."

"But don't you feel ashamed? I prefer to speak Chinese because I am Chinese and I don't want my children to forget how to speak it."

Duong leans forward, sips his beer. "Yeah, it's strange. You don't like to speak Chinese. And you are Chinese."

"No, I'm Canadian-Chinese. In Canada, being Canadian is an identity, not a race."

"*Ai-yo*, the Danes call us Danish," Andy and Duong laugh. "But that is bullshit. They don't treat us like Danes."

Corrina looks at her feet.

"Inside we are Chinese." Andy pats his chest. "It is pity if you don't speak your nationality's language."

"But my nationality is Canadian. I was born in Canada. My parents arrived in 1960."

Andy and Duong look at each other and laugh.

In the next room, Fong rocks her baby to sleep.

Vinni speaks on his cellphone. I tighten my grip on the beer can.

"Your skin is yellow, that mean you are Chinese. You need to stay with the culture. Are you too embarrased?"

"No," I say. "I just think it's good to have two cultures, integrate them." I purse my lips.

Andy laughs.

"I think you speak English because you want to be white. Being Chinese is a part of you. You should speak it and learn to use chopsticks properly."

My index finger and thumb turn yellow from my grip around the beer can. "I'm not obligated to be a certain way because of my skin colour. You're being just as prejudiced...."

"Okay, okay," Corrina touches my arm. "Jennifer is different...I always told you guys." She lightly taps my shoulder. "Let's go. We are taking you to the In-Club on Strongenblade."

Vinni takes my hand and we walk out the door.

"Have a good time," yells Fong in Danish as the heavy paint-chipped door slams behind us.

German techno blares as the black metal doors swing open below a pink and green sign that flashes "In-Club, Danish Pop." Danish girls line up to show their ID. Gel stiffens their styled, blond hair. Their earrings dangle and their makeup sparkles. The bouncer smiles and opens the door for four Danish girls. One of them is dressed like Britney Spears, her eyes lined with glitter gel.

Vinni speaks to his brother in Danish. Corrina tells me to get my ID ready.

"Tell him you are visiting from Canada." Corrina steps forward.

The bouncer pushes her back with one hand. He speaks in Danish. Corrina shakes her head and answers.

"What's going on?" I ask.

"Regulars only," says the bouncer.

"Do we need a membership card?" I ask.

The bouncer looks at the person behind me.

"Excuse me."

The bouncer ignores me again.

Vinni speaks softly to Andy and Duong. They back up.

Corrina pulls me aside.

My eyes dart from one person to the next. "What's going on?"

Corrina stares at the bouncer and speaks to Andy in Cantonese. Eight Danish girls pile through the door. I try to go in again, but the bouncer pushes me back.

"What do you want? You want to see my ID?" I speak loud and slow.

The bouncer shakes his head and closes the door.

I turn around.

Corrina, Andy, Vinni and Duong walk to the street corner and look on. Beside them wait Sikhs, Asians and Turks. The door swings open. The bouncer steps out. Andy approaches the bouncer and speaks with him in Danish.

Andy grabs my elbow. "We are going. We don't need to give them business."

"What's wrong?"

"The bouncer said they had troubles with some dark-haired persons earlier in the evening and he has strict orders not to allow any more in."

I shake my head. From the corner of my eye, I catch Vinni's hunched profile. He kicks the gravel near his feet in frustration.

"That's bullshit," I yell. I stomp towards the bouncer and grab the sleeve of his leather jacket.

"Excuse me."

The bouncer looks at me and continues speaking to a Danish girl.

"Excuse me," I repeat.

He ignores me.

"EXCUSE ME. I AM TALKING TO YOU!" I yell until my voice cracks.

The bouncer stares at me. The four Danish girls stop talking and look on.

"What is going on here? You are only letting in regulars who happen to be white. If this is a racial problem, then I will call the police," I say.

"You can call the police," the bouncer speaks in broken English. "They don't care. They do nothing."

"Then I want to speak with your manager."

"He will not come out. What is your problem lady? I am African-Danish, so don't fuck with me!"

"Vinni, call the police on your cellphone," I scream.

Vinni shakes his head.

"No, they will not come out for something like this," says Corrina.

I turn to face the bouncer.

"What kind of club are you running here? Aren't you embarassed you are living in a country that only respects you if you are nothing but a bouncer? This is pathetic...you should be embarassed." I clench my hands into fists. I shake.

Corrina smooths my arm and squeezes my elbow.

The bouncer turns away.

"Let's go, Jenn. They don't deserve our business."

"Asshole!" I yell.

Andy, Vinni and Duong follow behind.

Vinni puts his arm around me. "Don't worry, Jennifer, he nothing but a Nigger."

I freeze.

"That doesn't help," I say softly.

In Vinni's apartment, Duong pours each of us a shot of vodka.

"Sometimes it is difficult to be another colour in this country," says Vinni. "But you have to live with it."

Vinni laughs, his face already flushed from four shots of vodka.

"*Skhole.*" Our glasses clink.

"Shhhh," says Fong. "You will wake the baby."

I take aspirin for the headache I have from three beers and four shots of vodka. We wake up at 6 a.m., three hours after going to bed. My flight is at 8 a.m. Corrina drives me to the southern harbour on the way to the airport.

"I wanted to take you to Sweden, but since I threw up four times and you look like shit, I will take you to see the famous Copenhagen Mermaid so you can take some nice photos."

Copenhagen Mermaid

We stand on a rock and look out over the harbour lined with Danish sailboats. They float in the water, and, from afar, they look like miniature boats with their tall sails drifting slowly in the misty water. I drape a sweater over my shoulders.

"Does she look sad to you?"

"Sometimes. Depends on how you see her," says Corrina. "She is the symbol for Hans Christian Andersen's Little Mermaid and now we have her as the symbol for Copenhagen. She was modelled after a famous person's wife. I don't know who. Andy would know. He's smarter than me." Corrina brushes back the thick black strands of hair blowing into her face. "It's funny, her head was cut off in 1966 by some bad guys and then the city replaced it. Maybe that's why she looks so sad."

I hug my thick pink sweater. "The wind is so strong here. Even though you have more sun, it still feels like five degrees Celsius."

Corrina laughs, then shivers. "The cold winds started when you came."

"Very funny," I say.

"I hope you don't have a bad impression of Denmark. The Turks have it worse than us," says Corrina. "After two or three generations, they still own stores. Their parents do not encourage education and they let them run wild. They also have a strong religion that is difficult to integrate with the Danish society. They live in circles. At least the Chinese do not carry a strong religion and we work harder."

A horn sounds faintly from the Swedish ferry. Flags snap in the strong wind. We head towards the car.

"I am taking swimming lessons now," says Corrina.

"You never told me. Did you ever take swimming lessons when you were young?" I ask.

"No. I was helping at my parents' restaurant all the time. They depended on me and my sister to speak Danish and English when we had customers. But I am learning and someday I will swim just like a mermaid."

I laugh. "Like the Copenhagen Mermaid?"

"Yes."

Andy hands me my silver suitcase.

"I'll send some photos, but only if you promise not to post them on the Web," I say.

"Okay, but I'm not promising."

We hug.

Corrina hands me my plane ticket and purse. "Don't get lost in the Munich airport during your stopover, okay?"

I step onto the escalator and wave to Corrina. We wave until I can only see the tip of Corrina's fingertips moving slightly up and down. I turn and head for Departures.

Rosa Veltri

ROSA VELTRI, born in Toronto in 1976, the youngest of three and the only daughter to parents who emigrated from Italy in 1971, graduated from the University of Toronto with degrees in English, Professional Writing and History. Veltri now teaches grade school in Toronto and lives in Mississauga.

Maria Florentina

I came home from school and a blue and white For Sale sign stuck out of the lawn. I stood in front of the sign, pushed it with my hand and watched it swing back and forth. I ran up the wooden porch, opened the screen door and ran to the bottom of the stairs.

"Ma. Maa! How come we have that sign outside the house? Maa!"

Mrs. Sini, who lived on the first floor, marched toward me. "Why don't you go upstairs instead of yelling like a crazy?"

I waited until Mrs. Sini went back into the kitchen. I climbed up two steps and yelled, "Mom!"

My mother's legs appeared at the top of the stairs. "We selling the house."

I slowly walked up the narrow stairs. My mother stood in the kitchen steaming green beans she had picked from our garden. A picture of the Last Supper hung on the wall. In the left corner of the kitchen lay a mattress, two Barbie dolls and a trunk where I kept my clothes. My parents slept on the pullout couch in the family room. My brothers, Nick and Mike, shared the bedroom.

I tugged on my mother's apron. "Where are we going? Do I get my own room? Is it far away? Do I have to change schools?"

"Quiet!" she hissed. "We don't know yet. Now your father's coming home soon. Here's the beer. Go wait on the porch."

With two hands, I carried the brown, stubby bottle down the stairs and outside to the porch. I set it beside me on the bench and waited until I saw the blue Chevy pull into the driveway.

My father stepped out of the car carrying his green plastic lunch box in one hand. I got up, ran and jumped from the porch. He caught me with his free hand.

"Papa, where are we moving to? Is it in Toronto? Do I have to change schools? Are Nick and Mike coming with us?"

My father laughed. "You no want your brothers to come?"

I shrugged.

My father sat on the bench laughing. He put down his lunch box and picked up the beer.

"Papa, is it far away? Do I get my own room? Can I bring my bike?"

My father smiled at me. "Lotsa questions, eh? Papa doesn't know where we move yet. First we have to sell the house, okay?"

"Okay, Papa."

"Now go help your mother."

I went inside and my brothers, who had just come home from playing street hockey in front of Diego Borges' house, ran upstairs in front of me, fought over the remote, turned on the television and watched *The Dukes of Hazard*. I stood on a chair and took out five plates. I set them around the table. My mother dipped red strips of veal in egg and dropped the veal in a plate of bread crumbs. The oil sizzled as she placed the veal in the frying pan. Drops of oil hit the white wall. She poured pasta into a bubbling pot of water. I laid five forks, four knives and five cups on the table.

My mother stuck her head out of the kitchen.

Maria Florentina

"Nick! Mike! Time to eat! Go call your father!"

Nick and Mike pounced into the kitchen and bumped into my mother and me. Mike wiggled past Nick and sat down. Nick stood on the trunk, stepped on my Barbies, stuck his head out of the kitchen window and called down to my father. "Papa! Time to eat!"

Every day after dinner, Voula, Arathy, Vandevi and I took turns playing on each other's porches. If we felt like playing Barbies, they came to my house where I brought out my two Barbie dolls and the Barbie hairbrush. If we felt like playing Mr. Potato Head or the Hungry Hungry Hippo game, we went to Arathy and Vandevi's house. If we felt like playing skipping, we went to Voula's house because she had an orange, plastic skipping rope.

At school today, we had all agreed we wanted to play with the Barbies. Voula, Arathy, and Vandevi arrived as my mother and I finished drying the dishes. My brothers played Battleship in the backyard and my father watched television. I brought my two Barbies down to the porch. When I told them I was moving, Arathy and Vandevi cried, Voula asked me if she could have one of my Barbie dolls.

My father said we would move to Mississauga at the end of May. He said Nick, Mike and I would each have our own rooms, that we'd have to change schools and that, yes, I could bring my bike.

On moving day, my father and godfather lifted the table and chairs into my godfather's pickup truck and loaded in the boxes that didn't fit into the rental truck. My brothers rode with my godfather who drove the rental truck. My mother and I went with my father who drove my godfather's pickup truck. I sat on my mother's lap and watched Mrs. Sini wave and cry. The new owners had raised her rent seventy-five dollars.

As we approached the highway, my mother made the sign of the cross, turned and looked out the rear window. She sighed. In the back of the truck, the table wiggled and the top of one of the boxes opened and flapped. Two chairs slid against the table and my mother told my father, in a steady voice, to slow down. As we pulled into the gravel driveway of the new house, the rope holding the table and chairs snapped. My mother let out a final sigh.

My brothers and I stood and stared at the new house. Then we stampeded inside and dashed from room to room opening doors. We ran, stretched out our arms into the space, and twirled and slid on shiny hardwood floors. My brothers, searching for marbles, comic books and the soccer ball, ripped tape off boxes. I touched faucets, opened cabinets, ran my fingers across the grooves of the wood moulding and over nailheads visible through the white paint on the walls.

My mother held her chin with her hand and walked. She peeled the tape off boxes, peered at the contents and then moved on to the next box. She sat in a chair and crossed her arms and legs. She gazed at the door as if waiting for something to happen, for a show to start or for music to play. My father flung open the door, and with my godfather pushing on the other side, tried to squeeze the stove through the door. They put it down for a rest and my father stuck his head out toward my mother and said, "We got anything to eat? I'm hungry."

The new house had a kitchen, a family room, a dining room and a living room on the main floor and four bedrooms upstairs. The couch and the television filled the family room. The dining room

Maria Florentina

and living room remained empty. Upstairs my mattress, trunk and Barbie dolls took up a corner of my bedroom. My parents had bought themselves a new bed.

My first day at school I met Stephanie Gormon who was in my class and lived down our street. We took the bus to school with Ashley Johnson and Elizabeth Nimby. My mom said I could invite Stephanie over to play after school. We played with my two Barbies, changed their clothes and brushed their hair. My mother brought us some Orzata and Milano S cookies. Stephanie looked at the Orzata and held up the glass.

"Lucia, what is this?"

I looked at my mom and then at Stephanie.

"It's Orzata. It's made from almonds."

Stephanie sniffed her glass and then sipped.

I glanced at my mom.

Stephanie smiled. "That tastes good."

I smiled at my mom.

Stephanie put down her drink, "Lucia, after our snack, can we play with some other dolls or toys? Do you have the game Operation?"

I stared at my Orzata. "Uh, well my other dolls and toys are still in boxes. We didn't unpack them yet."

My mother peered down at me and walked back to the kitchen.

Stephanie went home after we ate our snack.

Keys jingled in the front door and I darted to the fridge to get a beer. I carried the beer bottle into the family room and then skipped to the door. My father picked me up and I kissed him on the cheek. He sauntered to the family room, sat on the couch and picked up his beer. I plonked beside him and told him that Stephanie invited me to her house on Saturday and that Nick and Mike wouldn't let me watch *The Smurfs* when I came home from school.

My mother walked me to Stephanie's house on Saturday and waited on the driveway until Stephanie's mother opened the door.

"Well, you must be Lucia. Stephanie's always talking about you."

Stephanie appeared at the door and grabbed my hand. I followed Stephanie upstairs to her bedroom. A white dresser, a white night table, and a white canopy bed furnished her room. A chain of stuffed toys hung from the ceiling. I counted twelve teddy bears, six dogs, three rabbits, two elephants, two pigs, a gigantic stuffed panda bear and a cow that said "moo" when I touched its belly.

Stephanie turned to me. "I just wanted to get my Operation game. I left it up here when Elizabeth came to play. Let's go to the basement."

I followed her to the basement and stopped in the doorway. Barbie's playhouse, Barbie's pink Corvette and nine Barbies filled one corner. A bookshelf and three shelves of games stood beside the Barbie playhouse. I walked to the shelf and saw Jenga, Hungry Hungry Hippo, The Telephone Game, Mr. Potato Head, Memory, Yahtzee and Monopoly on the first shelf. An Easy Bake oven, a Playskool cash register and a teacup set sat on the table. Stephanie removed the teacups, dropped the cash register on the floor and set the Operation game on the table. Behind me stood a pink baby carriage. I leaned over the carriage and looked at three dolls inside.

Stephanie skipped over to me, "Those are my Cabbage Patch dolls. You want to play with them?"

I nodded and she handed me one of the dolls. "Her name is Megan Lee Smith. You know how I know that?"

I shook my head.

"Because they come with a birth certificate, silly. See?" She pulled out a beige, rectangular card with a red seal stamped in the bottom righthand corner and black lettering: Megan Lee Smith.

I ran my fingers over the cool, crisp certificate and traced the grooves of the letters. Megan Lee felt soft. Her eyes opened and closed. Her blonde hair parted into two pigtails with pink bows. She wore a white dress with pink flowers and a lace collar.

Stephanie lifted Megan Lee's dress. "See? She has a diaper."

I played with Megan Lee until Stephanie wanted to play Operation. I put Megan Lee back in the carriage and covered her with the blanket. At one p.m., Stephanie's mother came downstairs.

"Okay you girls, time to clean up. We're going out for lunch soon."

Stephanie's parents dropped me off at home at three-thirty. Nick opened the door. "Where have you been?"

I rushed to the kitchen where my mother sewed patches on my father's work pants, and my father cut out coupons from the Canadian Tire flyer.

"Mamma! Papa! I went out for lunch."

They both looked up at me.

"It's true. I'm not lying. I ate Chinese food."

My brothers strolled into the kitchen. Mike scowled, "How come she gets to go out for lunch?"

I faced him, "I went with Stephanie's parents."

Nick and Mike chimed in highpitched voices, "I went with Stephanie's parents," they mocked as they left the kitchen.

I faced my parents again.

"Ma, Stephanie's parents let me pick what I wanted from a cart. There were so many carts Ma. I used chopsticks—well I tried but the food kept falling, so they gave me a fork. Ma, the place was so nice. They served us and we didn't have to clean dishes or nothing."

My mother nodded and threaded her needle. My father clipped coupons.

"Ma, look, I brought the napkin because I knew Mike and Nick wouldn't believe me." I showed my mother the napkin.

My father set down the scissors, plucked the napkin out of my hand, crumpled it and threw it in the garbage. My mom tied a knot and cut the thread with her teeth. My father left to sit in the family room.

After ten minutes he yelled, "Lucia! Get Papa a glass of wine."

I lifted the bottle of wine, poured it into a glass and brought the glass of wine to him.

The following Saturday, I went to Stephanie's house to watch the movie *Ghostbusters*. When I walked in, Stephanie's dad put the dishes in the dishwasher and Stephanie's mom put a bag of popcorn in the microwave. Stephanie and I sat in the family room and Stephanie's mom joined us. Stephanie's dad swept the floor. The movie started and I stared into the kitchen and watched Stephanie's dad wipe down the counter and bring a tray of drinks for Stephanie's mom, Stephanie and me. In the middle of the movie, I turned around and Stephanie's dad held a beer. Stephanie hadn't moved and neither had Stephanie's mom.

"How did your dad get that beer? " I whispered to Stephanie. "Does he do that all the time? Aren't you or your mom supposed to get it for him?"

Stephanie laughed. So did her parents.

Stephanie turned to her Mom. "See Mom, I told you Lucia was funny."

The next day my father's keys jingled in the door and I sat on the couch and watched *G.I. Joe* with my brothers.

"Lucia!" my father called out my name. Nick and Mike looked at me.

My father came into the family room. "Hey Lucia, what's matter with you? Are you sick? You no hear me? Where's my beer and no hello, no hug, no nothing? You sick?"

Nick and Mike wrestled on the floor. "Give me the Hulk Hogan card. I'll trade you for Macho Man Randy Savage or Andre the Giant. You had Hulk Hogan all last week."

"Hi Daddy," I said.

"Give Papa a kiss." He sat beside me, and I kissed him on the cheek. He yelled at my brothers. "No fighting, and change this channel. Go to the news." He winked at me. "Come on, go get Papa a beer."

I stood up and stared at him.

"Come on fast, Lucia, go. What's wrong with you today? Go get my beera."

I held my hands behind my back and blurted, "Get it yourself Daddy."

My brothers went still. I winced as the back of my father's hand hit my cheek. I cried. My father rested one hand on my shoulder and with one finger underneath my chin, lifted my head.

"You call me Papa. No Daddy. I'm Papa."

I cried. He picked me up, carried me to the fridge, got his beer and then carried the beer and me back to the couch. He sat me down on his lap and placed the beer on the coffee table.

"How come you no want to get beer for Papa, eh? You no love Papa anymore?"

We sat silently and watched *G.I. Joe* and *The Smurfs* until my mother came home.

We ate spaghetti and meatballs for dinner. I rolled the meatballs and my mother dropped them in the sauce. Nick amd Mike played outside, and my father watched television. I set the table and my mother asked my father to call my brothers for dinner. We sat down for dinner and my father told me to go get him a glass of wine. I poured the wine and brought it to him.

Before going to bed, my mother tucked me in.

"Lucia, how come you talk to your father like that today? How come you didn't want to get him a beera?"

I turned onto my side.

My mother shook my leg, "Come on, what's matter with you?"

I faced her and cried. "Ma, Stephanie's dad gets his own beer and Stephanie never has to get it for him and you know what? He even got drinks for us." I wiped my nose on my pajama sleeve. "It's true. He brought us drinks in the family room. Stephanie never has to get her Papa anything. He gets it himself."

My mother went to the washroom to get Kleenex and told me to blow my nose. "Ma, how come we have to do everything? Why doesn't Papa help?"

She pushed my hair away from my face and smiled at me. "Maybe when you grow up be different, but now is like this. Can't change now."

"Ma, it's not fair. Nick and Mike never have to help and—"

My mother pressed her finger on her lips. "Shh. Go to sleep. Only beginning of what's not fair. I hope is different for you. When you grow up, you change what you want, okay? Now is like this." She kissed me on the forehead. "Go to sleep." She got up and turned off the light.

I missed Stephanie's birthday party at Chuck E Cheese's. Stephanie brought a piece of cake and a loot bag to school for me. The next week at recess, she told me how she and Elizabeth played Jenga and The Telephone Game on Saturday. On the last day of school, Stephanie showed me pictures of *Grease on Ice*. Stephanie said that she gave my ticket to Ashley Johnson, and that Ashley complained that she was cold the whole time. At the end of the summer, Stephanie asked me to go to Florida with her and her parents. She said we could go to Disneyland and go on all sorts of rides. I asked my father and he said no. Stephanie's mom called my mom, but my father still said no.

I begged my father as he measured a wall in my room. "Please Papa. I can go see Mickey Mouse and the dolphins and go on rides and go to the beach."

My father left the room. I heard my parents talk in the kitchen.

During his two-week vacation from the factory, my father worked construction with my godfather. My mother and I picked and washed six bushels of tomatoes. We laid them in the garage until they turned red. My father brought home two bushels of peppers that my mother and I roasted and peeled. We pickled and jarred the peppers, a bushel of eggplant and a bushel of dill pickles. When the tomatoes ripened, I helped my mother cut the tomatoes, boil them, put them through a machine and jar the sauce. I got a postcard from Stephanie with Mickey Mouse and Goofy on the front. At the end of the two weeks, my godfather drove my father home in his pickup truck. The back of the truck held a brown dresser and bed frame. My father and godfather carried the dresser and bedframe to my room and set them up.

School started again and my birthday approached. I circled the picture of the Cabbage Patch doll in the Consumers Distributing catalogue. It looked exactly like Stephanie's Megan Lee. The dress was white with pink flowers and a lace collar. Two pink bows tied her blonde hair.

The caption above the doll in the catalogue read, "The even softer Cabbage Patch doll!"

The doll came with a birth certificate, diapers and eyes that opened and closed. I kept the Consumers catalogue in my room until twelve days before my birthday.

My mother washed dishes at the sink. I dragged a chair to the sink, tapped my mother's shoulder and held out the Consumers catalogue.

"Mamma, you know my birthday is in twelve days."

My mother glanced at me. "Oh, yeah?"

"Yeah, Mamma and I know what you and Papa can buy for me."

My mother scrubbed the saucepan.

"A Cabbage Patch doll. See?" I pointed to the picture in the Consumers catalogue and imagined my Cabbage Patch doll sliding out of the plastic curtains onto the wheely counter at Consumers.

"Ma, it comes with a birth certificate and diapers." I patted my mother's shoulder. "Don't worry Ma, I'll change the diapers, okay? You won't have to do it, I promise. Besides, it's just pretend, Mamma, she doesn't really go to the washroom. I promise I'll do it."

My mother wiped her hands on her pink-and-blue-flowered apron. "Let me see dis book."

I held up the Consumers catalogue. "Ma, Stephanie has three Cabbage Patch dolls and a baby Cabbage Patch doll too, but don't worry Ma, I only want one. I don't want three. Too many diapers to change."

My mother held the book close to her face.

"*Aya marona*, sixty-three dollars for one doll. You crazy. Pick something else in the book."

She whipped the catalogue onto the counter.

"But Ma."

"No. Is too espensive, pick something else." She dunked her hand in the dirty water and fished for the green scouring pad.

I snatched the catalogue as I stepped down from the chair. I ran to the family room where my father sat watching a soccer game. I placed my hands on his knees, pushed myself up and sat on his lap.

"Papa."

"Ssh." He pointed to the television.

"Papa."

He "ssh'ed" me again.

I grabbed his face with both hands and looked straight into his eyes.

"Papa, do you know it's my birthday soon?"

My father smiled and said, "Who's birthday?" He leaned his head to the right to see the television.

"Papa, it's my birthday very soon. It's in twelve days. Can I have this doll?" I pointed to the picture in the catalogue. "Please Papa."

My mother yelled from the kitchen. "I already tol her is too espensive."

I wrapped my arms around my father's neck and rested my head on his shoulder, "Please, Papa."

My mother yelled again, "Is too espensive. Stop asking your father."

I looked up at my father. He winked at me and whispered, "We see." In a loud voice he said, "Go help your mother. I watch soccer now."

My birthday arrived. My mother said we would have cake in the afternoon. A big box with orange-flowered wrapping paper sat in the middle of the table. I tore the wrapping off and stared at a plastic doll in a pink and blue flowered dress, with a plastic face and painted on eyes. On the back of the doll's head, a big bald spot showed through two thin pigtails made out of yarn. I tapped the bald spot.

Nick blurted out, "Mike and I glued the hair, but we ran out of string."

My father tugged the doll's dress, "You like the dress, huh, you mother made it exactly like the picture in the Consumer book."

I looked up and my mother smiled. I stared at the doll's face.

My mother laughed. "Your father paint the face. He maybe stare at the picture for two hours, but did a good job—no?"

I lifted the doll's dress.

My father patted my head. "Hey, you no like the doll. I thought this was the doll you want. Look like the one in the book—no?"

I stared at the black yarn glued on the plastic head. I lifted the doll's dress again, "Where's the diaper?"

My father laughed. "A diaper?"

"Yes, Papa, it's supposed to come with a diaper and a birth certificate."

"No, it no need diaper, Mamma already toilet trained her." My mother laughed.

I peered up at my father. "But they're all supposed to come with diapers."

My father waved his hand in the air. "Who says? This one is toilet trained. It don't need diaper, so why you need diaper?"

"Where's the birth certificate?"

My father laughed. "Okay, you want birth certificate. I get it for you."

Maria Florentina

My father went down to the basement, came back with a brown cardboard box. He tore one of the flaps off the top and grabbed a red Crayola marker from the kitchen counter. "Okay." He winked at my mother. "Letta me see. We name her Maria, okay." He wrote Maria on the cardboard in capital letters.

My mother laughed.

My father tapped his chin with the marker, "Letta me see. Maria, we need a last name…ah, Maria Florentina." He wrote Florentina in capital letters beside Maria. He held up the piece of cardboard, "You like, eh?"

I giggled. "Papa, you have to write the day Maria was born."

He winked at me, "Okay, borna." He picked up the marker again and wrote October 22, 1983 on the cardboard. "Okay, Lucia, now we baptize Maria."

My mother snorted and spit out her wine.

My father called for my brothers who had slipped into the family room to watch the *A-Team*.

"Nick, Mike, come here. You two are the godparents, you baptiza Maria."

I giggled again and my father carried me to the sink and sat me on the counter. He turned on the sink faucet. My brothers watched the *A-Team* and my father yelled, "*Oh ma vagabondi*, I call you."

Mike and Nick looked up.

"Get over here!" my father yelled.

My brothers strolled to the kitchen sink.

My father pointed at Mike. "Hold Maria."

Mike scowled, "This is stupid."

My father glared at my brothers and they each held one of Maria's legs. I held her head.

My father straightened his back and cleared his throat. "You boys repeat after me: 'I promise to looka after Maria.'"

My brothers mumbled. "I promise to look after Maria."

My father pointed to Nick. "Puta little water on Maria's head and kiss her cheek."

Nick flicked the stream of water coming out of the faucet. Water sprayed Maria.

My father cleared his throat again, "I hereby decree Maria Florentina, born October 22, 1983, is baptizata."

My brothers dropped Maria's legs. "Can we go now?"

My father waved them away and touched my nose. "Okay, now you like Maria." He picked up Maria and held her in front of me, "Now, you love Maria, right? No hurt her feelings. She's gonna cry."

I snatched the doll from him. "Yes, Papa. I love Maria."

"Good girl. Now me and you going to have a big piece of cake."

I sat on my father's lap as my mother passed us a piece of cake with two forks.

For the next three weeks, I took Maria to the grocery store, to the park and to the washroom. At night, Maria slept beside me.

One day at school my teacher, Mrs. Bingman, announced my turn to bring something in for show-and-tell. The next morning I wrapped a blanket around Maria so she wouldn't get cold and tucked her in my school bag with her birth certificate. Show-and-tell time was always before lunch. Mrs. Bingman said she wanted us to explain why the thing we brought was special.

Ashley Johnson went first. She brought in three Barbies and Barbie's pink Corvette. Ashley stood up straight and said, "My Barbies and Barbie corvette are special because I love Barbie and I love the colour pink." Ashley seated the Barbies in the Corvette and wheeled it once around the classroom.

Next, Kyle McDirk showed his Transformer Optimus Prime. Kyle said, "Optimus Prime is so special because it is the best transformer and it turns into a truck." Kyle transformed Optimus Prime into a truck and held it up for the class to see. He let Joshua Lipton wheel it around the room.

My turn came. I brought my school bag to the front of the class. I took out the birth certificate and placed it on the desk. Then I took out Maria Florentina, laid her on the desk, unrolled the blanket and held her up to the class.

"This is my Cabbage Patch doll."

Mrs. Bingman waved her hand, "Lucia you have to speak up. The class can't hear you."

I started again. "This is my Cabbage Patch doll and her name is Maria Florentina. She is special because—"

Ashley Johnson laughed and raised her hand. "Mrs. Bingman. Mrs. Bingman. Lucia's lying. That's not a Cabbage Patch doll. It's plastic."

Mrs. Bingman stared at me. "Lucia, is that a Cabbage Patch doll?"

I nodded.

Ashley yelled, "No, it's not. I have four Cabbage Patch dolls and they don't look like that. Where's the birth certificate?"

I picked up my birth certificate and held it up in front of me.

Ashley scowled. "That's a piece of cardboard. There's not even a stamp on it. You're lying. Plus what kind of name is Maria Florentina? That's not a Cabbage Patch doll."

Joshua yelled out, "Maybe it's an Italian cabbage patch doll. It's a wop doll. That's why it's so ugly. It doesn't even have hair."

The whole class laughed. I rolled Maria up in the blanket.

Kyle grabbed the birth certificate and yelled, "You just wrote this with marker."

The class laughed again. The lunch bell rang and Kyle dropped the birth certificate on the floor. Three people stepped on it. I shoved the certificate in my school bag and Mrs. Bingman called me to her desk.

"Now, Lucia, if there is one thing I will not put up with in my class, it's lying. You shouldn't try to pretend to have something you don't. You should be grateful for what you have. Now after you eat your lunch, you come back here. There will be no recess for you."

I ate my lunch in the washroom. After lunch I went back to the classroom and wrote out "I will not lie" across the back and front of three pieces of paper. After school, instead of waiting for the bus with the rest of my class near the portable, I hid in the tube slide at the park until everyone left, and then I walked home. After two blocks, I saw my brothers riding their bikes toward me.

Nick yelled from across the street. "Lucia, where have you been? Why didn't you get on the bus?"

Mike braked an inch from where I stood.

"You know you got us in trouble. Papa was going to kill us for not making sure you were on the bus. Let's go."

He patted the handlebars. I stood still. Nick shook my shoulder. "What's wrong with you?"

I cried. "They called me a liar. They said Maria was fake and ugly. They stepped on my birth certificate."

Mike rolled his eyes. "Well, don't cry. Let me see." He opened my school bag and yanked out my birth certificate. "It'll come off, it's just dirt." Mike rubbed the birth certificate against his leg. "See? The dirt's gone. Let's go. Papa's going to kill us."

I continued to cry. Mike slipped the birth certificate back in my school bag. Nick picked me up and sat me on the handlebars of his bike, "Stop crying. Me and Mike will beat them up tomorrow, okay?"

Mike slid my hood over my head, pulled the strings tight and tied a bow. My brothers peddled towards home. They stopped at the convenience store and bought a Tootsie Roll, saying I could have it if I stopped crying. I finished the Tootsie Roll before we got home.

My father waited by the door. When he saw us, he walked outside, picked me up and carried me inside. "What happen to you, eh? You miss the bus?" A shred of toilet paper stuck to my father's cheek and shaving cream smeared the skin near his right ear.

My brothers walked in.

My father glared at them, "From now on you make sure your sister's on the bus before it leaves and if she's not on you get off and find her. You tell the bus driver to wait. You have to look out for your little sister. You no come home without her."

He looked at me, "Good thing you home before your mother or we all been in trouble." He scanned my face, "You cry. You scare. No worry, you home now. Next time you go to the principal office, okay?"

I nodded.

He set me down and took my school bag from me, "Oh, this is heavy, what you have in here?" He opened my bag and took out Maria Florentina. "Why you have this big blanket in here?"

I stared at the bald spot on the back of Maria's head and looked up at my father. "In case she got cold."

My father laughed. "Oh ya, today you bring Maria to school, eh? How they like Maria?"

My father knelt on one leg. He tried to straighten Maria's pigtails and smiled. I rested my head on his shoulder. He smelled like Aqua Velva and soap.

My father yelled at my brothers. "You know as godfathers you're suppose to look after Maria. Next time you make sure her and Lucia are on the bus."

My brothers watched television. My father grinned and held out Maria. I grabbed Maria and stared at her plastic face. I stared at her pink dress with blue flowers. I stared at her bald spot.

My father winked and tickled me, "So, your class, they like Maria?"

I stared at my father's face. I stared at the shred of toilet paper that still clung to his cheek. I stared as my father re-tied the pink bow around Maria's pigtail. "Yes, Papa. They liked Maria."

Cotton Undershirt

The first day of grade seven I walked to school. My knapsack hung heavily on my back. My right hand grasped the rolled up edges of the brown-paper-bag lunch that my mother packed that morning: a peanut butter sandwich, an apple, a nectarine, a grape drinking box and three homemade, chocolate chocolate chip cookies. On the front of the lunch bag, my father had drawn a happy face in black marker.

I scurried past the grade-eight boys and girls and skipped toward Chrissy, Claudia and Rachel who huddled around the back of portable nine. Chrissy wore lipstick and had dyed her brown hair a golden blond. Rachel wore a short shirt so her belly button showed and Claudia had teased her bangs. Outlines of bras showed through Chrissy, Rachel and Claudia's T-shirts. I wore the pink-flowered cotton undershirt that my mother had bought at Bi-Way on sale, two for $4.99. I turned my lunch bag so the happy face pressed against my thigh.

Rachel rambled on about some high school boy she met at the Valleys Community Centre during the summer break. She explained how they kissed in the park beside the monkey bars. Chrissy and Claudia giggled and nodded. I giggled too and glanced down at my new white running shoes. What does frenching mean and where exactly did Rachel let him stick his finger?

Tipper's Fruit Market

The phone rings and I dash to pick it up.
"Hey, guess what?" Katie says.
"What?"
"My mother talked to the manager at the fruit market and we got the jobs. We just have to go in."
"Are you serious?"
"What can I say? My mother's got connections."
"You're not shittin' me?"
"No."
"You want to walk there today?"
I meet Katie at the corner. She wears the Red Hot Chili Peppers T-shirt I bought her for her birthday. I gave her the T-shirt two days before her fourteenth birthday. I thought it might make her feel better since her party got cancelled.

We carried the can of beer in a brown paper bag to the video store and rented the movie *The Doors*. We took turns sipping the beer on the walk to the store. In the video store, Katie hid the can in her jacket. We took turns sipping the beer on the walk back to Katie's house. When we got to Katie's, we placed the half-full beer can in the centre of the coffee table in the family room, on top of a pile of books. We sat cross-legged, sorted through a bunch of old tapes and sang along to an old Corey Hart favourite. We belted out the chorus:

I wear my sunglasses at night, so I can, so I can—

The front door opened. We stopped singing. I stood up and dropped the cassette I held. Katie slammed the glass door to the stereo shut. I stared at Katie; Katie stared at me. Her father stood in the doorway and stared at the coffee table. The can of beer sat on top of the pile of books. Katie swallowed and we stared at the floor. I gave her the Red Hot Chili Pepper's T-shirt the next day.

"So, been listening to any Corey Hart lately?"

"Shut up." Katie smiles. "How long do you think it will take to walk there?"

"Beats me. It only takes five minutes with the car."

"We should probably stop for provisions. Just in case."

We stop at a convenience store and buy two jumbo freezies—one red, one blue—and two sour keys. We walk down Caper Road sucking on sour keys and slurping our freezies.

"How much do you think we'll get paid?" I ask.

"My mom said minimum wage."

"How much is that?"

Katie shrugged. "Four twenty-five an hour."

"Shit. Is that all?"

"Yeah. So what are you going to buy with your first paycheque?"

"Black ten-hole docs. How about you?"

"A stereo for my room."

Tipper's Fruit Market

I laugh and snort. Katie laughs and points to red freezie liquid that runs down my chin. We cross the street at the Caper and Kingsdale intersection. Cars honk in the parking lot of Tipper's Fruit Market as a delivery truck backs up.

The automatic doors of Tipper's Fruit Market slide open. Katie sticks out her blue-stained tongue at me. I wash sticky, red freezie liquid off my chin with my spit. Bushels of apples line an aisle that opens into the produce section. A pitch fork, nailed to the wall, hangs above the two doors at the back. Dark wood panels the walls of the fruit market. A row of four cash registers stretches beyond the produce area. Five blond cashiers wear green smocks with red apples on the front. They cluster beside one cash desk talking. A boy in a Montreal Canadien's T-shirt stacks bananas. A sign near the strawberries reads, "Homemade Jam." I smell pie.

Katie and I walk by the broccoli, celery, romaine and iceberg lettuce stands to the back of the produce area. Katie knocks on the swinging doors that lead into the back room. A scrawny woman with short blond hair pushes open the door with one foot. She squints at us. Brown blotches stain her red apron and hard pieces of white dough cling to the apron.

Katie clears her throat. "Um, hi. My mom came in here earlier and, um, she said you guys needed people."

"Oh yeah. Great. Come on in." We step into the back room. The woman smiles and her skin creases around her eyes and mouth.

"Just fill out these applications. I'll be right back with Joanna. My name's Cindy. I'm one of the managers. Joanna and Mike own the place." Cindy hands us each a pen and an application. "I'll be right back."

A man, with dark curly hair and a moustache, stands near a garbage bin behind us. He husks corn and stares at us. Cindy licks her chapped lips. "Don't be scared of Frank." Cindy grins and steps out of the back room.

The man husks the last corn in the bag and walks into the produce cooler.

Cindy and a woman with chin-length blond hair return before Katie and I have filled out the applications. Cindy stands two steps behind Joanna. Two inches taller and three inches wider, Joanna eclipses Cindy. She wears a pink Polo golf shirt and tight blue jeans. Baby blue eyeliner rims her eyes and pink lipstick glosses her lips.

"Hi there," the woman says. "I'm Joanna. So I hear you girls are looking for work."

We nod.

"Well, for right now, I need one of you for cash and one of you for the bakery. And your name is?" Joanna looks at Katie.

"Katie."

"Katie, I love your strawberry blond hair."

"Thanks."

"You must get that a lot."

Katie smiles.

"Well, Katie, do you have any cash experience?"

"No, I've only babysat before."

Joanna studies my face. "And you? What's your name?"

"Rosa."

"Ah, Rrrosa." Joanna laughs and waves her hands in the air. "Have you had cash experience before?"

"Yes, I worked cash at a doughnut shop."

Joanna takes my application then gazes at Katie.

"So how old are you girls?"

"Fourteen," we say.

Tipper's Fruit Market

The phone rings. Joanna looks at Cindy, who answers the phone. They both nod.

"Okay." Joanna sighs, "Well, you know weekends are very busy here, so we expect you to work weekends."

Katie and I nod. Joanna peers at me and points to Katie.

"Katie, you can start tomorrow on cash. When you come in, look for Cindy. She'll train you." Joanna scribbles on the applications and waves to me with her left hand without looking up.

"You can start tomorrow too. Go see Michelina in the bakery when you come in." Joanna scans the applications.

Katie and I say, "Bye, see you tomorrow."

No one answers.

We step out of the back room and stroll down to the bakery, where a stocky, dark haired woman sweeps the floor. I slide a cherry danish into a white paper bag and stand in front of Katie as she slips the bag underneath her T-shirt. We hurry by the cashiers and out the door.

Katie tries to push the danish up and out of the bag without losing the cherry filling. "Ro, I can't believe we're going to be making our own money. This is so cool."

I nod. We halve the danish and walk home.

Katie rambles on. "I wanna get a whole bunch of CDs for my new stereo. I wanna get the new Stone Temple Pilot CD—I heard the preview on CFNY and it was amazing. We should go to the flea market on Saturday, I wanna trade in my Guns and Roses CD." Katie sucks cherry filling off her thumb.

My eyes follow a crack in the sidewalk. I wonder why Joanna laughed when I told her my name.

Katie and I start work the next day at 4:00 p.m. Katie follows Cindy to the cash area. I walk to the bakery to find Michelina. A woman with short brown hair and pink-framed glasses sweeps the bakery floor. The broom handle stands a foot taller than she does.

"Hi. I'm Rosa, it's my first day. Joanna said to see Michelina, is that you?"

She points at me with the broom handle, "What is your nama?"

"Rosa. Joanna hired me yesterday."

The woman sighs, "Yeah—I Michelina. You work for me in bakeria?"

I nod.

Michelina shakes her head and waves one hand in the air.

"Always someone new they send me. Okay—you sweepa the floor. I leave soon. I send Amy to come help you. Another day, I teach you. Now I go home." Michelina takes off her apron and ambles out of the bakery. A woman taps on the bakery counter with her long fake nails.

"Two butter tarts and a small meat pie."

I smile at the customer and gently place two butter tarts in a white bag and a small meat pie in a brown bag. I smile again, "There you go, ma'am. Have a nice day."

Michelina leaves for home at 4:10 and sends Amy to the bakery to train me. I serve the customers. Amy changes the stickers on the pies, so the date reads June 14 instead of June 10. Today is June 11. A tall lean man walks around the store. He stops in front of each aisle and then each department.

"Amy, who's that guy?"

"Oh, quick. Look busy."

Amy grabs a rag from the sink and wipes the counter; I slice two loaves of rye bread for a man with a comb-over.

"So Amy, how long have you worked here?'

Tipper's Fruit Market

Amy's long loose blond ponytail swings as she wipes the counter. "About three years. I'm quitting in August. I'm going to Humber College in September, so it's good riddance to this place." She laughs. "You're my replacement."

A woman with a teddy bear pin on her coat clears her throat.

I smile. "Can I help you?"

"Three custard tarts and a Nanaimo bar."

I place the items in a white cardboard box.

"Amy, how much are Nanaimo bars again?"

"Fifty-nine cents each."

I write the price on the box. I turn to ask Amy how much custard tarts cost; Amy's not behind me. The tall, lean man stands near the sink with his legs spread two feet apart and his arms by his side. He wears a green sweatshirt with "Tipper's Fruit Market" printed in black letters around a red apple. Grey streaks his short, light brown hair. He points at me.

"You don't know how to read?"

"Pardon?"

"The prices are on the front of the counter. Is it so hard to go walk around to the front of the counter and check the prices?"

"Uh, it's my first day."

I walk around the counter and squeeze my way through the customers that stand in front of the bakery counter.

"Excuse me," I say. "Excuse me, I just need to get by to check the prices."

The lady I serve yells out, "Sixty-nine cents. Custard tarts are sixty-nine cents."

I squeeze through the crowd and walk back around the counter. The tall lean man still stands by the sink. He watches me change the stickers on the pies, wipe down the counter and sweep the floor. As I bend down with a dust pan to sweep up the pile of dirt, I glance up and he's gone.

Amy reappears.

"Where did you go?"

"I was in the freezer."

"In the freezer?"

"Yeah, Mike gives me the creeps." Amy shivers.

"You mean that guy that was here? Is he a manager or something?"

"No, Mike owns the place. What did he say to you?"

"Nothing much. He just stood there."

"Doesn't he give you the creeps?"

"Yeah, sort of."

"Whenever he's around, make sure you look busy."

Amy changes the garbage bag and drags it across the floor to the back door.

"I'm going to bring the garbage to the bin. It's just out here."

She points at the door. I fold boxes. A man in a leather jacket and gelled hair stands near the bakery counter. He coughs and smiles.

"Is it too late to get a quiche?" he says.

"No, just a second." I package the quiche.

"Do you have any bagels left?"

"Yes, right over there."

I turn and see Mike standing near the bagel bin, his hands on his hips. Two girls and a boy in blue and white school uniforms run down the bakery aisle. Joanna strolls behind them. The boy, a six-year-old, scampers in front, sliding on the balls of his feet around the bakery counter. He snatches a brownie, scurries through the deli

Tipper's Fruit Market

and out of sight. A tall, lean eight-year-old girl grabs two custard tarts, one in each hand and waits beside the bakery counter. A chubby-ten-year-old girl reaches for a butter tart.

"Cynthia. Put that back." Mike steps into the bakery.

Cynthia stands still. "Hillary and Ritchie took treats," she says.

"You never mind."

"But, Dad, I'm hungry."

"So, get yourself an apple," Mike says. "You don't need any treats."

Joanna walks into the bakery. Cynthia glares up at Joanna.

"Mom. Hillary and Ritchie got treats."

Joanna reaches for a butter tart. "Really, Cynthia, you don't need a treat." Joanna bites into the butter tart. "Go ask Frank to cut you up some fruit. They've got pineapple." Joanna takes another bite. "You like pineapple."

"Did I hear my name?" The man who husked corn yesterday stands in the bakery.

Hillary, crouched beside the bakery counter, tugs on Cynthia's kilt. Cynthia inches away from Joanna and retreats with Hillary into the deli.

"Frank, just the man I'm looking for," Joanna says. "You guys making fruit salad in the back? Cynthia's got the munchies." Joanna waves to where Cynthia stood. "Oh," Joanna laughs and turns to Mike, "these kids."

I fold boxes and study the grain in the woodwork counter.

"She new?"

I feel Frank's finger pointing at me.

"Yeah." Joanna nods my way. "I hired her yesterday."

Mike stands in front of me on the other side of the work counter. Katie jogs down the bakery aisle.

"Joanna, we need you to sign an invoice."

I smile at Katie. She smiles back. Frank looks at Katie.

"She new too?"

Joanna nods, "Yeah. They're friends."

Katie follows Joanna back up to cash. My back faces Mike and Frank.

I scrub a muffin tray in the sink as Frank talks to Mike.

"Those watermelons we got in last week were all shit. Three customers returned them already. You should call and cancel the next order."

I rinse the tray and pick up another one.

Frank sneezes. "I ordered another skid of corn this morning. Got that special on peaches and cream this weekend. Sold really well last weekend. You want me to put the sign back up outside?"

Mike grunts, "Wouldn't mind fucking that."

I turn my head and glance up. Mike's eyes trace my body. Frank shoves his hands in his pockets. I look away.

"Uh, yeah." Frank mumbles. "So, do you want me to put that sign outside?"

Mike and Frank continue to talk. I scrub the muffin trays. I scrub the sink and the faucet. I scrub the plastic holder for the scrub pad. I hold the scrub pad underneath the water until the water runs clear. A woman's voice says, "Excuse me." I turn my head slowly and see a woman leaning against the counter. I flick my head to the left and right. I turn off the faucet and peer down the bakery aisle. Adjusting my apron, I walk to the customer. "Can I help you?"

The Bakery

My bike wobbles as I chain it to the fence behind the fruit market. Flattened boxes tied with string lie on the ground outside the back entrance. I yank my balled apron out of my school bag and slip it around my neck. I walk into the bakery at 3:56 p.m., just as Amy drops a mouldy muffin into the garbage pail. She swings around when she sees me.

"Well it's my last day and I only have four more hours in this hell hole." Amy runs on the spot and waves her hands in the air. "Well, Rosa dear, I wish you luck. Don't look so worried. Just stay out of Mike and Frank's way. Do your job and you'll be fine."

"Am I going to be by myself in here?"

"Yup. Michelina wants you to work Saturdays. You start at seven. Saturdays are really busy. You'll be Michelina's helper. She bakes the pies, muffins and cookies in that oven behind you. Just do what she says. The bread, buns, quiches and stuff are baked upstairs and sent down on this pulley." Amy kicks the pulley rack. Steel baking trays shake and clang against the rack. The pulley rack, six-feet tall, stands on four wheels. Black patches of grime grease the rack and hardened flecks of dough stick to its sides. Twenty empty trays rest on top.

"Okay, so here's how the pulley rack works. A lever upstairs moves it up and down, so if you want the baker to pull the rack up or if you want to talk to the baker, you shake the rack. He'll poke his head down to see what you want. If the baker jerks the rack once, that means yes. If he jerks it twice, that's no."

I look up. A cord tied to a metal ring attaches the rack to a pulley in the upstairs bakery. I turn to Amy.

"It's so dark. Who works up there? Who's the baker?"

Amy's eyes open wide. "Nobody knows."

"What?"

"It's true. I've worked here three years and I've never seen the baker. I've heard him, but I can never understand what he says. Veronica says he never comes down because he's deformed like the elephant man in that old movie." She shrugs. "But then Mona says it's this old man that walks with a cane."

I laugh. "That's so stupid."

Amy shakes her head. "All I know is that I've never seen him, her, or whatever it is that works up there. Do you know Raheem and Justin? They work in the back room. You'll meet them soon enough. One time Raheem dared Justin to climb the ladder to see who was up there, but Frank saw him climbing the ladder and yelled at him to get down. No one's allowed to go up there without Mike or Frank's permission. They think we'll hide up there instead of working."

I package a quiche for a customer and Amy sweeps the floor. As the customer leaves, Amy nudges me. "Let's go upstairs and find out what the baker looks like. It's my last day. What are they going to do, fire me? Besides, you're new, you can just plead ignorance."

The Bakery

Amy grabs my sleeve and pulls me to the back door of the bakery. The back door leads into the back room. Amy scans the room, looks back at me and mouths, "Follow me." Amy scurries to a wooden ladder and climbs. She stops at the top of the ladder, pokes her head down and whispers, "Come on."

I climb up. Amy and I each have a foot on the top step of the ladder. Our heads and shoulders jut through a hole in the ceiling.

"Amy, I don't see anything. It's so dark. No one's up here."

Amy sighs. "Yeah, that sucks. But I wonder if there's a light switch?" She stands on tiptoe.

"You girls get down from there!" The ladder shakes. We both look down at Frank, who shakes the ladder. "Get down right now, before Mike sees you!"

Amy and I glance at each other. Amy slowly climbs down the ladder and I follow.

"What the hell were you girls thinking? You're not supposed to be poking around up there! Not to mention you could've cracked your heads! You're lucky Mike didn't see you." Frank faces Amy. "You know better than that, Amy."

"But Frank, it's my last day. We were just goofing around. I wanted to know what the baker looked like. I've nev—"

"The baker? The baker's not here. He starts at four in the morning and leaves before you've even rolled out of bed. Now get to work, Mike's comin' any minute now."

We walk back into the bakery. I wash muffin trays and Amy fills the brownie tray.

Amy sighs. "I met the cutest guy at my college orientation. He's in my business program. I hope we have some classes together." Amy fills a small bucket with soapy water and grabs a scouring pad.

"I'm kinda freaked out though. Just from the orientation, college seems like it's going to be sooo much work. No time for riding anymore. Do you ride?"

I shake my head no as I dry my hands on my apron. Amy scrubs the oven and I fold boxes. "I love riding." Amy grins. "I wanted to be a professional equestrian, but it's just not practical, you know? I even had my own horse." Amy smiles at me. "His name was Clarence. He was so cute. I got him when I was six. You should have seen him. He was gray and had three black spots on his nose."

"You don't have your horse anymore?"

"No, my parents sold him. I mean it just wasn't practical, you know." Amy dunks the scouring pad in the bucket. "They sold him and gave me the money to go to college." She squeezes the scouring pad and water drips into the bucket. "But I got to ride him that whole week. Anyway, you know, it just wasn't practical."

Amy scrubs the grimy grey oven until it shines. I stack boxes underneath the counter. Amy leaves at eight o'clock. I watch the hands on the clock until eight-thirty.

The next day, I walk into the bakery at 7:02 a.m. and Michelina points to a tray of cherry danish pastries. "Ice-a the danish."

A brush sits in a bucket of icing. I pick up the brush, wipe the handle and spread icing over the danishes.

Michelina waves her hand at me. "You in school."

I nod.

"How old are you, fourteen?"

I nod again.

The Bakery

"Ah, fourteen. Too young. You know my son stay in school long time too. He teacher. Yeah—all that money and he no even like. He teach one year and that's it. Says children mean, don't listen. He quit. Now he home watch TV. All that school to watch TV." She sighs, waves her hand and makes the sign of the cross.

Michelina scoops muffin batter out of pails into muffin trays. The pulley rack squeaks and scrapes the side of the wall as it comes down. I twirl the brush in the icing. Michelina slaps my arm.

"No daydream. Take trays off the rack and put-a in the oven."

She points to the pulley rack and hands me a pair of oven mitts. I lift all the trays from the rack into the oven. Michelina walks over to the oven. "Okay, listen. You finish, you shake the rack one time so he pull back up. Okay?"

I nod.

"Now put bread in the bag, okay?" She points to a box of plastic bags.

I put the loaves of bread in the bags.

Michelina sighs. "He never make enough-a whole wheat." Michelina waits as the pulley rack rises and comes down with two trays of quiche and four trays of cheese buns. Michelina bangs on the side of the rack and yells, "Futi! Futi! Need-a more whole wheat!"

The pulley rack jerks.

Michelina turns to me. "You see, if he say-a yes, he move one time this rack. If he say-a no, he move two time. Okay?"

I nod and wrap the quiches with Saran Wrap. A short plump man stands in front of the counter. His sweatshirt rides above his waist so his pink belly peeks out. I step forward. "Can I help you?"

He glances up and shakes his head. He steps back and stands behind the bread baskets.

Michelina whips her head toward him and yells, "Vincenzo. I come." She turns to me. "That my son." She puts her coat on. "Yeah—too bad you so young. You nice girl, you could marry my son." She smiles.

I look up at the bread baskets and her son is gone.

Michelina slaps my back. "Okay bye—no forget to turn off the oven."

Magda, the deli manager, walks into the bakery when Michelina leaves. Magda bangs on the side of the pulley rack and yells, "Freddie! Freddiiee! Make me some fresh cheese bread to take home and don't burn it!"

The pulley rack jerks twice.

Magda curses and I hear a man chuckle. I scurry to the side of the rack and look up. I see a dark outline and I hear more chuckling.

Magda pushes me out of the way, bangs on the pulley rack again and yells, "Freddieee!"

The pulley rack jerks once.

I walk into the bakery at 6:58 a.m. and Michelina lies on the floor. Her left hand grasps the bottom wheel of the pulley rack. Her right hand presses on her lower back. I rush to her.

"Michelina, are you okay? What happened?"

Michelina peers at me. "Disgraziato." She points to a sausage roll flattened and stuck to the sole of her shoe. A pink sponge roller slips out of the navy-blue-flowered handkerchief tied around her head. I hold out my hand. "Here, let me help you."

"No. No. I cannot move."

"Do you want me to call an ambulance?"

The Bakery

"No. No. Call my son. Call Vincenzo." She recites the phone number as I press the numbers on the phone. She moans. "Ay, I have my niece wedding tonight. Disgrazia."

I hang up the phone.

"No one's home, Michelina. I'm calling the ambulance."

She shakes her head as I dial 911. She moans and bites into her left arm.

I squat beside her. "They're on their way, Michelina."

A pink sponge roller bounces up and down when she moves her head. I roll her hair back around the roller and push it underneath the handkerchief.

Michelina sighs, "Ah—too bad you're not older."

The ambulance arrives fifteen minutes later. The paramedics lift Michelina onto a stretcher and wheel her out of the store.

Mike walks into the bakery and tells me to bake the muffins, cookies and pies.

I slide a tray of cookies onto the first oven rack, two trays of banana muffins onto the second rack and two trays of bran muffins onto the third rack. The fourth and highest rack in the small oven stands a foot over my head. I stand on tiptoe, swing my head back from the heat of the oven, reach in with oven mitts and feel for the rack. I place six frozen apple pies on a tray, stand on tiptoe and hold the tray up over my head. I lean into the oven and raise the tray higher to reach the fourth rack. The tray slips and the pies slide off the tray. My left forearm bangs against the edge of the hot, steel oven racks. I scream and drop the tray.

The pulley rack jerks.

I hold my forearm and squeeze my eyes shut. "Shit, shit, shit." A long pink bubbly rectangle of skin, the size of a lighter, rises where my forearm hit the edge of the oven rack.

The pulley rack jerks three times.

I squat and stare at my forearm. I see a mouldy muffin wedged between the floor and the bottom of the oven. Five aluminum pie shells lie upside down on the floor. Pieces of frozen pie crust and apple filling leak from beneath them. I squeeze my left wrist and bite my lower lip and groan.

The pulley rack jerks four times.

I stand. Yellow and white flakes cling to the edge of the oven rack where my forearm hit. The sixth apple pie squishes in the crevice between the oven and oven door. Apple filling melts and dribbles to the floor. I squat and squeeze my wrist.

A hand touches my shoulder. A Vietnamese man with short, black hair and a scar above his right eye squats beside me. He smiles. Small yellow teeth peek out from his lips. He wears a stained, white apron over a white sweatshirt with a red stripe across the front and baby-blue jogging pants. He points to me, grabs my left hand and yanks my arm straight. I turn my head and squeeze my eyes. He chuckles. I open one eye and watch as he taps the skin around my burn. He pulls a brown pouch out of his apron, takes a leaf from the pouch, walks to the sink, wets the leaf and returns. I dig my nails into the palm of my hand as he places the leaf over my burn. He walks to the bakery counter, returns with four pieces of scotch tape and smooths them over the leaf and onto my skin.

He stands up and holds out his right hand. I reach for his hand and he yanks me up. I stand a foot taller than him. The last apple pie slides from the oven to the floor. Apple pie filling and pie crust splatter across the floor. The man chuckles, looks up and shoves the brown pouch in his apron pocket. He points to himself. "Fudi," he says, "My name Fudi."

I smile.

The Bakery

Fudi smiles back and slips out of the bakery.

I walk into the fruit market at 4:05 p.m. Cathy, the night manager, pokes her head around a cash register.

"Don't go burning yourself today, Rosa," she says.

I walk into the backroom. Frank talks on the phone.

"Barb, I'm going bowling with the guys tonight, so don't wait up."

I punch my card in. Frank hangs up the phone. He yells from where he stands. "I hear you shake-and-baked your arm." He walks over to me. "Did it scar?"

I hold out my left arm and show him my burn.

Justin carries a box of bananas out of the cooler and stops beside us. "Oh, cool. Did that hurt?"

Frank looks at Justin. "No, it tickled." Frank looks at me. "Didn't anyone tell you you're always supposed to wear long sleeves when you use that oven?"

I look up at him. "No. No one told me."

Frank laughs. "Oh."

"Hey Frank," I say, "How's Michelina?"

"How should I know?"

I roll my eyes and walk to the bakery.

I serve the customers, fold boxes, clean the bakery counter twice, sweep the floor three times and build a pyramid of paper baking cups. The phone rings. I continue to build my pyramid. On the fifth ring I pick up the phone.

"Hello. Tipper's Market, Bakery speaking."

A soft, high-pitched voice says, "Can I talk to my mom?"

"Who's your mom?"

I hear nothing. I wait.

"Cathy."

"Okay. Just a second."

I walk up to the cash area. Kelly sits on cash number four and Annie stands beside her. They eat sour candies from a plastic container.

"Anyone seen Cathy?"

Mona smirks. "Find Frank, you find Cathy."

I walk to the backroom. Justin whips grapes at Raheem. A grape bounces off the right side of my head and Justin yells, "Sorry, Ro!" He ducks under the counter.

A grape bounces off the left side of my head. Raheem's head pokes out from behind a stack of boxed of oranges. "Sorry, Rosa."

Justin's hand pats the counter top for loose grapes.

"Get out of the way, Ro. It's a war zone."

I crouch behind a shopping cart full of broccoli. "You guys seen Cathy? You guys seen Frank?"

Red and white grapes whiz by me.

Justin and Raheem yell, "Out back."

I walk past Nelson, who slides elastics around loose stems of broccoli. I turn the corner to the delivery area. Two figures lean against the wall. A woman has her legs wrapped around a man's waist. The man leans his head between her neck and shoulder. The woman giggles.

I turn around. I hear shuffling.

Frank yells, "Who's there?"

I swallow. "Ah…the phone's for Cathy. It's her son."

"Who's there?"

"Ah…it's just me…it's Rosa. Sorry, ah…it's just that Cathy's son is on the phone. Do you want me to tell him you'll call back?"

"No!" Cathy hollers. "I'm coming."

The Bakery

I hear the zip of a zipper. I walk back into the backroom. Cathy walks behind me. Raheem grabs a broom and sweeps. Justin stands up from behind the counter, grabs a price gun and prices bottles of salad dressing. Cathy struts pass me to the phone. I bolt into the bakery and take down the pyramid of paper baking cups. I sweep the floor twice. My broom hits something under the oven. A green mouldy muffin rolls out from underneath. I sweep it into the dustpan and drop the mouldy muffin and dirt into the garbage bin. I Windex the glass front of the bakery counter and wipe the fingerprints away. The strings of the mop stick to the floor as I mop. I gather the left side of the black garbage bag in my left fist and the right side of the garbage bag in my right fist. I yank the bag up and out of the garbage bin. The mouldy muffin pops out and drops to the floor. I tie the corners of the bag in a knot and kick the mouldy muffin back underneath the oven.

Christmas Party

Katie and I sit on milk crates in the bakery, and eat our Kriss Kringle gifts. I got a Mickey Mouse mug full of jelly beans from Veronica who works up at cash with Katie. Katie got a box of Turtles from Mona in the deli.

"I wish I had a chance to change." Katie wears her green school kilt.

Magda, the deli manager, pierces sticks into rolled veal for the party.

"You girls. Young ladies. Up, up. Here—carry this tray upstairs, and you, take the potato salad."

Magda will leave with her daughter and grandchildren for a vacation in Acapulco after New Year's. "Two weeks of heaven." Magda's eyes widen. "Sun, beach and no kolbasa to be seen."

When I started working at Tipper's Fruit Market in June, Magda said that in the twelve years she had worked at the fruit market, she had never seen anyone squish bread like me.

"You have to be gentle with the bread. You make the bread look like a collapsed bridge! Who's gonna want to buy that, huh? You put the bread in the bread slicer gently, then hold the handle while the machine slices. Don't drop the handle! What do you think, you're chopping wood?" Magda shook her head, sighed, tugged on her apron and handed me another loaf of bread. Magda gazed out at the deli counter. Five people waited in line. Magda shifted her weight to one foot and laughed.

"Magda, what's so funny?"

"Ah, nothing." She glanced at me. "You're too young to understand." Magda shifted her weight to her other foot. "You know I remember when this market first opened. There were no customers. So one time Joanna, Mike and I came up with this idea on how to get customers to come in. We dressed Mike up like a chicken."

"What?"

"Yeah. Joanna and I—this was when she already had Cynthia and was pregnant with Hillary—oh, how they wanted a boy that time, but some things you can't control. Anyway, where was I? Yes. Joanna and I stayed up all night sewing this chicken outfit. You can't imagine the work, gluing all of those feathers on. The next day Mike put on the chicken suit and stood outside near the road holding a sign that said **FRESH PIES** on one side and **FRESH FRUIT** on the other. That day I think maybe we sold twelve pies and three bushels of apples. Ah, wasn't much, but it was a start. Look at this place now."

Seven customers waited in line at the deli and the pie stand needed to be refilled.

"You," Magda said, "why you laughing?"

"I'm still picturing Mike dressed up like a chicken."

Magda laughed, too. "Ah, he wasn't always a bully."

I slipped the sliced bread into a bag and grabbed another loaf.

Katie, Magda and I climb the stairs and go in the upstairs apartment for the first time since we started working at Tipper's Fruit Market seven months ago. We pass by the kitchen and office and

Christmas Party

step into a long room with a bar at one end and a television at the other. Katie had heard Veronica say that Mona overheard Joanna tell a customer that she and Mike used to live up here before they had kids. Veronica also said that Mike and Joanna just built a huge new house not far from here. When I suggested at Halloween that we drive by and egg the house, Veronica said I would need a pretty good arm because it was a mile from the road.

Frank, the produce manager, stands behind the bar writing TIPS on a plastic cup with a black marker. Katie sets her tray on the table; I set the potato salad on the bar counter.

"You ladies want a drink? What can I get you—wine spritzer, martini?"

Magda sets down her tray and says, "White wine. The good kind, don't be stingy."

Frank looks at me. "Wine spritzer?"

I nod. "Sure."

He hands me a wine spritzer and looks at Katie. "Same for you?"

Katie blurts out, "Got any Molson Export?"

Mike walks in and Frank looks up. Mike smiles and says, "You girls help yourself, the beer's in the fridge."

Katie walks to the kitchen. I follow and knee her in the back of the leg.

"I can't believe you said that. I didn't think they were going to let us drink. Maybe he doesn't know we're only fifteen. Maybe you shouldn't take it. Maybe he was joking."

Katie laughs and shrugs. "Hey, he told us to help ourselves." She opens the fridge. "And that's what I intend to do."

I giggle as she struggles to open the beer bottle.

"Maybe it's not a twist cap. Maybe you need a bottle opener."

Katie rolls her eyes and points to the words TWIST CAP on the top of the cap. She wrestles with the cap.

I laugh and throw a dishcloth at her. "Here, try using that." She drapes the dishcloth over the bottle, twists the cap and opens the bottle. "Voila." She kicks the fridge door closed.

"Yeah, it only took you five tries."

She kicks me in the shin and I spill some spritzer on my shirt.

"Hurry up and finish your spritzer. We've got a whole fridge full of beer."

We walk back into the long room. Magda sits on a stool near the bar talking with Mike and Joanna. The deli ladies huddle in the corner. Veronica and Mona sit on the couch with paper plates on their laps. We sit on the floor near the television with Dan and Raheem. Dan and Raheem work part-time in produce. Peter, the only male cashier, walks in and sits beside Katie. Katie, Peter and I take turns going to the kitchen to get beer. Dan and Raheem sit with their backs to us, drinking pop.

Dan nudges Raheem. "Can you believe some of these people? Look at how they're drinking."

Raheem slaps his thigh and adjusts his baseball cap. "Dan, Dan. Look at Joanna. She's on the floor laughing."

Dan combs his fingers through his hair. "So?"

"No, literally on the floor. Ha! Ro, look at this." Raheem turns around as I swig my beer. "Ah, Rosa not you too."

Dan turns around. "Rosa. Where did you get that?"

Katie drinks from her bottle, but she misses her mouth and spills beer down the front of her shirt. Peter lies on his side and laughs. I spit up my beer on Dan.

"Shit—Ro! Shit, you guys are psycho."

Peter sits up. "Relax Dan, it's just beer."

"You guys shouldn't even be drinking beer in the first place."

Peter rolls his eyes. "Oh Jesus, like you've never drunk beer before."

"No. I don't smoke or drink."

Peter slaps his back. "Well, don't take it out on me."

I feel nauseous and crawl under a coffee table.

When I wake up Frank is shaking my leg. I raise my head and hit it on the top of the coffee table. Frank lifts the coffee table and I crawl out.

"Whatsamatter with you? Get up. Katie looked all over for you."

I lose my balance and stumble.

"Rosa! Get up! If your parents see you like this they're going to kill you and me and Mike and probably anyone else they can get a hold of. Get up!"

Frank slaps my cheek three times and wraps his arm around my waist. Joanna sleeps with one arm dangling off the coach. Mike sits at the table and grins.

"So, it was you girls that cleaned the fridge out." He laughs.

Frank walks me to Dan's car. Katie and Peter sit in the back. Katie snores and Peter sings: "Take me down to Paradise City, where the grass is green and the girls are pretty. Ohh, please take me home."

"Dan, you sure you're okay to drive?"

"Yeah, Frank. I didn't drink anything. I don't drink."

"You know where they live? Make sure you drop the girls off first and drive careful."

"Sure thing, Frank. Don't worry."

I wake up to Dan yelling.

"Katie! Come on. Get up. You're home! Pete, you're not helping."

Peter sings, "Ohh pleease take mee ho-omme."

I step out of the car.

"Ro! Rosa! Get back in the car. Where are you going?"

I shake Katie's shoulder. "Katie—it's Ro. You're home." I shake her shoulder again.

Katie opens her eyes and smiles. She mumbles, "Where are we?" I smile. "You're home."

Katie slowly lifts her legs out of the car. She throws both arms around my neck and I pull her up. Katie stumbles and Dan grabs one of her arms and swings it around his neck. Dan and I guide her to her door. I fish for her keys in her coat and open the door. Dan waits outside. I guide Katie to her family room and she lies on her couch. When I walk out of Katie's house, Dan still stands outside the door.

"Shit—is she okay? See? See, this is why I don't drink. You guys are crazy."

Peter thrusts his arm out the car window and bangs on the car door.

"Let's go, Dan. I feel sick! Take me home!"

"Pete, stop. You'll wake up the whole neighbourhood."

I walk to the car and continue past it.

"Rosa. Where are you going?"

"Home."

"What? Wait I'll drive you."

"Thanks, Dan, but I feel like walking."

"Shit. You guys are so crazy."

Peter bangs on the car door again. Dan hops in the car and follows me home. He drives so slowly that when Peter has to puke, he just opens the car door and sticks his head out. A trail of light brown chunky puke starts at the Chinese Presbyterian Church and ends on my driveway. I unlock my front door and Dan waves.

The next week at work Magda marches toward me.

Christmas Party

"I can't believe you girls. Drinking like that. Because of you, that was the last Christmas party Mike and Joanna are having." Magda huffs. "Do you know that Veronica's parents called to complain? I can't believe you girls. These days I can't tell anymore. I used to think you were a nice girl." She hands me a piece of paper and a pencil. "Here, write down the names of Mike and Joanna's kids. I'm a horrible speller. Never get it right."

I hold the paper and pencil, "Why?"

"None of your business." Magda wipes the counter with a damp rag and looks at me, "I want to bring them T-shirts from Acapulco with their names on it. Can you imagine if I spelt their names wrong? Mike would never let me forget it. He always teases me about my spelling."

Antoinetta takes over as the deli manager when Magda leaves for vacation. After two weeks I ask Antoinetta when Magda is coming back. Antoinetta shrugs.

After three weeks I ask Edyta, who works in the deli, "When's Magda coming back?"

Edyta cuts salami.

I tug the green flowered scarf that she always knots around her neck, "So when's Magda coming back?"

Edyta guides the salami into the slicer. "Ah, Rujia. This is garbage you know."

"What?"

"They left message on machine. Told her no come back. Can you believe?"

"Excuse me, this bread is ruined. I would like another loaf."

A customer holds out a loaf of bread pinched in the middle and bubbled out on each side.

Edyta grabs another loaf of bread.

"Aya Rujia, you do. I always squish."
"Here. Come Edyta, I'll show you how."

Half a Case of Oranges

Black crows perched on black garbage bags turn their heads as I ride my bike down Caper Road. I whiz by freshly cut lawns and plastic planters filled with pink and purple impatiens and orange and yellow marigolds. My jean shorts cling to the backs of my thighs. Crazy Patty stands on the corner of Caper and Kingsdale Roads, pushing the crosswalk button. I start work at 7:00 a.m. It's 6:58. The white lines of the road, empty of cars, glare in the sun. I want to ride through the intersection, even though the red hand flashes.

The last time I crossed when the red hand flashed, Patty yelled as I rode by. When the light changed she crossed the street, barged into the grocery store, eyes glazed, waved her finger and sputtered, "Red means stop. Red means stop."

I slow as I near the corner and set one foot on the pavement.

"Good morning, Patty."

Patty's pink jogging pants ride high above her waist and expose a chapped, pink patch of skin on her shins between the elastic cuffs of her pants and the tops of her socks. She glances up at me and presses the crosswalk button. I stand on my pedals and grasp the handle bars. Patty waves her index finger an inch from my nose as she gazes at her feet and yells, "Red means stop."

I set both feet on the pavement, lean my elbow on my handle bar and rest my chin on my hand. Patty shoves her long bangs behind her ears and pushes the beige frames of her glasses to the bridge of her nose. She presses the crosswalk button over and over and over with her index finger. She places her left thumb over her right thumb and leans into the button, breathing out with every push.

I check my watch—7:03 a.m. The stoplight turns yellow. I hop onto my pedals. The stoplight turns green and the white neon man replaces the red flashing hand. I bolt across the intersection, swerve between delivery trucks in the parking lot to the back of the grocery store and chain my bike to the fence.

I stroll to the side door and step into the back room. The deliveries have arrived. A skid of watermelons sits in front of the cooler. Flattened cardboard boxes fill a wooden crate. A ribbon of loose lettuce leaves, grapes, plastic bubble wrap and orange peels trail around the cracked plastic garbage bins. Edyta stands on a two squares of carpet and sorts strawberries at the counter. She winks at me. Frank, the produce manager, stands near the punch clock. He scratches his ass.

"Hi, Frank."

"You're late."

"Sorry."

"There's an order for fruit salad. Get started. They'll be here at ten to pick it up."

I drag a damp rag across the wooden counter, pushing potato peels and cooked macaroni to the floor. I wash the fruit salad bowl and cut up three cantaloupes, half a seedless watermelon, a pint of strawberries and ten kiwis, sliced half a centimetre thick. Edyta fills green, square cardboard containers with strawberries. I bump her as I walk by. Edyta smiles and reveals three missing teeth on her lower gum. Two gray whiskers poke out of the mole beside her left eye. I lift two honeydew melons out of a box and carry them back to the counter.

Frank hoots, "Nice melons, Rosa." He slips into the storage cooler.

Edyta leans one elbow on the counter and yawns. She throws an empty cardboard box in the bin and picks up another box from the pile beside her.

I stand over the garbage bin and scoop out the seeds of the honeydew melon with a spoon.

"Hey Edyta—"

She swings around and holds her red-stained hands up like a doctor before surgery.

"Is your daughter coming from Poland?"

Edyta grins. "September, Rujia. Cheaper in September." She swings back around and plucks five strawberries from the counter and examines each one. Edyta takes a bite out of the fifth strawberry and tosses the other four strawberries into a green container.

Justin rushes in through the swinging doors that lead to the store as I slice the honeydew melon into squares. He wears a Bart Simpson T-shirt. A new cluster of pimples sprinkle his forehead.

"Hi Ro."

"Hi Justin."

"Where's Frank?"

I point to the storage cooler.

"Frank. Frank!" Justin's voice squeaks and cracks.

With the knife, I push squares of honeydew off the cutting board into the bowl. Frank trudges out with his hands on his hips. His small pot belly pokes over his waistband. Edyta stands straight and examines each strawberry before she places them into the container.

Frank hollers, "What?"

"How much is a case of oranges? A lady wants to know."

"Same price they were yesterday when you asked me."

Frank pushes the plastic curtains aside and stomps back into the cooler. I drop a handful of blueberries into the bowl. Justin shifts his weight from one foot to the other and readjusts his baseball cap. I drop two more handfuls of blueberries into the bowl.

Frank hollers, "$14.99."

Justin takes off through the swinging doors. His voice rises and squeaks through the store.

"It's $14.99, ma'am. Would you like a case, ma'am?"

I stare into the fruit salad and snack on cantaloupe pieces. Frank comes out of the cooler and claps his hands.

"Rosa, let's go! The customer's going to be here at ten!"

He strides into the washroom and leaves the door open. Frank adjusts his starchy new Blue Jay World Series T-shirt and combs his fingers through his hair. I pluck grapes off the stem and drop them into the bowl. He walks to the counter under the phone and flips to page 3 of the *Toronto Sun*.

Frank whistles and croons, "Melanie, oh sweet Melanie."

He grins, rips the page out of the paper, then walks over to Darryl. Darryl shifts in his tight, black wrangler jeans as his dry, cracked hands wind an elastic around a head of lettuce. Frank hired Darryl, his brother-in-law, when Loeb closed down. On his first day, Darryl horked in the garbage bin next to me and said hello.

"Hey Darryl, look at this babe. Her name is Melanie. Her hobbies include swimming and horseback riding."

Darryl grins and drops the head of lettuce into the cart. He crosses his arms and tugs on his mustache with his right hand. "She can ride me any time."

Half a Case of Oranges

Frank and Darryl laugh and drool over the picture.

Justin rushes in through the swinging doors. "Frank, the lady only wants half a case of oranges. Is that okay?"

"No."

"Why not?"

"'Cause I say so."

"But she only wants half."

"Yeah well, I only want a new car. Tough."

"I don't see what the big deal is. Why can't I sell her half? That's all she wants and I already said it was okay."

"Are you trying to tell me how to run this store? I've worked in a grocery store since I was seventeen! Do you think you know more than me? You sell her half a case, then you have to cater to everyone! Half a head of lettuce, half an apple. No way!"

Justin clenches his teeth. "Well, you go explain it to her!"

Frank flips through the *Toronto Sun* and then shakes his head and grunts. "Where is she?" He tacks the picture of Melanie to the corkboard on the wall and follows Justin out to the store.

Melanie, a tanned, long-haired blonde, wears a white bikini. Her pink, pouty lips match her pink nails and pink stiletto heels. Beside Melanie hangs yesterday's Sunshine Girl, Amber. Amber's fireengine red hair falls in ringlets around her face. Her tiger-print bikini matches the tiger printed stool she sits on. Amber's crossed legs dangle to one side and her hands grasp the edge of the seat. Chrissy and Jennifer pose beside Amber. In the bottom left-hand corner a thumb-tack pins a wallet-sized picture of Frank's baby daughter to the board.

Frank returns to the back room. He puts half a case of oranges in a box and marks the box $6.99. He thrusts the box into Justin's stomach. Justin grasps the lower corners of the box.

"Oh sure, Frank, I thought we weren't allowed to sell half a case." Frank grins, rams his thumbs through his two front belt loops and yanks up his pants. "Well," Frank glances at me, lifts a bag of corn and drops it onto a cart, "let's just say a good pair of tits will take you places."

Rolling my eyes, I fill clear, plastic containers with fruit salad, weigh and price the containers. Frank shoves an empty cardboard box between the scale and me. I stack ten containers of fruit salad in the box for the order and place the rest on a tray. I carry the tray out to the store and ram the containers into the ice on the display counter. Frank walks by and claps.

I turn to face him.

"Rosa, let's go. Potatoes need to be filled."

I follow him to the backroom. Edyta sorts through strawberries. I grasp a bag of potatoes with both hands and carry it to the potato bin. I slice the bottom of the bag open with a knife and watch the potatoes roll to the bottom of the bin. I straighten the bags of bean sprouts and sweep the corn husks on the floor into a pile. I walk into the back room, grasp another bag of potatoes with both hands and carry it out to the bins in the store.

A Heater and a Fan

Simon, one of the stock boys, shaved his head over Christmas. His bare head surfs the cans of sauerkraut at the top of the canned goods aisle and bounces up and down as he mops. His pants hang three inches above his ankles. Simon turns into the bakery aisle, leans his mop against the bun bin and walks toward me. He flicks his head to the left and then to the right and pushes his glasses up with his index finger.

"So, what do you think about a union?"

"A union." I raise my eyebrows.

"Ya. I'm going to start a union. You interested?"

"Can you do that? Can you start a union, just like that?"

"Well, I have to get people's signatures first."

"I'll sign."

"That's cool, but I really need the full-timers to sign too. You're pretty close to some of the older deli ladies. Maybe you could talk to them about it."

I Windex the glass of the display counter. "Sure, but they're going to ask me what they'd get out of it. Do you know what the union offers?"

"No, not yet. But I'm looking into it. I got lots of ideas. Maybe we could ask for full benefits and paid lunches. I don't know how you've put up with this place for so long. How long have you worked here? Three, four years? That's nuts. Man, it would be so cool to stick it to that Mike. So far I've got three full-timer signatures—me, Katrina and Joyce—and five part-timers. Six if you sign."

I tear paper towel off a roll. "I thought you were part-time. How do you go to school and work here full-time?" I wipe the glass in circles.

"I don't go to school. I dropped out. They were trying to institutionalize me. Conform me, you know what I mean? I'm working here for now. In the spring, I'll work at this organic farm."

"Organic farm?"

"Yeah. Everything is grown naturally. Do you know how many chemicals you're eating by buying the vegetables from this store? Pesticides and God knows what else."

Someone shuffles down the aisle. "Anyway, we're meeting with the union guy tonight at seven-thirty. You want to come?"

"Sure. Where?"

Simon writes down directions and grabs the mop. Frank strolls into the bakery.

"You almost done here?"

"Ya. I just have to take out the garbage."

"Was Simon bothering you?" Frank peers at Simon. "Cause I know that kid's a little weird."

"No."

"All right. Well, hurry up." Frank strolls out of the bakery. "Some of us want to go home."

It's 7:42 when Kristine and Sarah drop me off in front of the long brown building.

A Heater and a Fan

"Okay," Kristine blurts, "so explain to me one more time why we're dropping you off here and picking you up later."

"This guy Simon I work with is trying to start a union. They're having a meeting tonight and I want to hear what they have to say."

"A union. What do you care about a union? I thought you were quitting at the end of the summer."

"I am." I button my jacket. "But I told Simon I'd stop by. I don't know, I kinda want to hear what it's all about."

"Okay," Kristine whines. "We'll go get the movie tickets and meet you back here. You better come out when I honk, 'cause I don't want to be late for the movie."

I step out of the car and Kristine and Sarah drive away. Brass trims the glass door to the building and black letters across the door read:

UFCW

Underneath, smaller letters read:

UNITED FOOD AND COMMERCIAL WORKERS' INTERNATIONAL UNION LOCALS 175 AND 633

I pull the brass handle and step into the building. Voices echo from the end of the grey corridor. Yellowed newspaper articles in black frames hang on the wall:

LOBLAWS UNIONIZED

UFCW WINS THE VOTE

ZELLERS U-NITED

Paint peels around the doorway of the office. A black poster dangles from a thumbtack on the opened door, white lettering across the poster reads:

THE 'U' IN UNION IS 'YOU'

Katrina and Simon sit on grey chairs at a round grey table. Katrina drinks coffee; Simon drinks pop. A tall, fat man stands in front of a chalkboard. He wears a plaid dress shirt and brown corduroy pants. He has a full beard and the top rim of his glasses sits above his eyebrows. He points to the words written on the chalkboard with a ruler and speaks.

"I guar-en-tee your work environment will improve one hundred percent with a union." He points to the word ENVIRONMENT. "I guar-en-tee better wages." He points to the word WAGES. "I guar-en-tee you'll get benefits." He points to the word BENEFITS and faces me.

"Well, looks like we got a latecomer. Come in. Come on in. You don't have to stand at the door. Come on in and grab a seat. My name is Bill and I'm your union rep. Help yourself to doughnuts and pop."

Simon passes me the box of doughnuts.

I take a rainbow-sprinkled doughnut and sit down.

"What's your name there, sweetie?"

"Rosa."

"Alrighty. Well, Rosa, here's some union cards and pamphlets for you to read." Bill hands me a blue pamphlet, a white pamphlet and a green pamphlet. "Katrina and Simon wrote out a list of complaints. Why don't you read the list over, grab the pen and see if there's anything you'd like to add?"

Katrina slides a clipboard to me but keeps the pen. I read the list of complaints and flip through the pamphlets.

"Alrighty. Is there anything you want to add?"

"Um, I can't think of anything else right now."

A Heater and a Fan

"Alrighty. Well, are you free this Saturday? I'm taking Katrina and Simon out for dinner. You're welcome to join us. Leave your phone number and address. I'll call you tomorrow and you can let me know." Bill taps his ruler against his thigh. "As I've told Katrina and Simon we need sixty percent of the workers to sign union cards. That means we need about twenty-seven to thirty signatures to get things rolling. The most important thing is to sign up as many people as you can."

Kristine and Sarah honk.

"Okay. I'll try." I blurt. "I'm sorry, but I have to go."

Simon glares at me and rolls his eyes.

"Alrighty, thanks for coming out." Bill smiles. "You know it always makes me proud to see young folks trying to better things for others. So you get as many signatures as you can and we'll see you on Saturday."

Katrina and Simon gaze at the chalkboard. I scurry out of the office with my stack of union cards, pamphlets and rainbow-sprinkle doughnut. Kristine drives up and honks her horn again. I see my reflection in the car window.

I jog down to Caper Road and Kingsdale. I cross the street and stare at the wood-panelled fruit market. Cars weave through the packed parking lot. Mike and Joanna pull up in a cherry red Cadillac. Across the street, Edyta and Wioletta step off the 3B bus. Edyta waves to me and I wait for them to cross the street. Edyta wears a long purple and black polyester skirt and gray running shoes. Wioletta wears the pink jogging suit with the flowered collar that she has worn all week. We walk into the fruit market, put on our aprons and punch in. Mike's voice filters through the store.

"Pick this shit up from the floor!"

Annie holds a broom and stares at a dustpan near her feet.

"Are you stupid or something? Leaving a pile of dirt in the middle of the store like that." Mike turns to walk away.

Annie clenches the broom handle. "I was going to pick it up. I just—"

Mike wheels around. "Clean this shit up right now!" He glares at her.

Annie bends down and sweeps the dirt into a dustpan. Mike stomps into the backroom. Annie drops the dustpan and cries and runs to the washroom. Kelly sweeps the dirt into the dustpan, dumps the dirt into a garbage bag and runs after Annie.

Wioletta and Edyta walk to the deli. Darryl and Frank step out of the backroom and Frank tugs on my shirt.

Darryl jerks his chin at me. "What happen to Annie?"

"Mike yelled at her for not sweeping up a pile of dirt fast enough."

Darryl shakes his head. "What an azzhole that fuckin' guy is. Yous know what that fuckin' azzhole said to me when I asked him for a raise? Says he has to think about it and I haven't seen one fuckin' cent. Azzhole knows my wife's pregnant. How am I suppose to support a kid and a wife on ten bucks an hour? If I could I'd fuckin'—"

"Darryl," Frank whispers. "Mike's still around, eh." Frank winks at me. "Plus, Rosa doesn't want to hear you bitchin'."

Darryl mutters and storms into the backroom. I walk to the bakery.

A Heater and a Fan

That Friday at the fruit market, I sign up five people. On Saturday, I go to Kristine's boyfriend's cousin's house party. On Sunday, Simon calls me at home.

"So thanks for gracing us with your presence on Thursday and stiffing us on Saturday."

"Look, it's just—"

"I thought you were for the cause. Never mind. Did you get any signatures?"

"Ya, so far I got five."

"Oh. Okay. Well I got four and Katrina got three. Wow, this is cool. We're halfway there. Hey listen, you know this is hush hush, right? If Mike, Joanna, or even Frank found out, they'd probably fire us or start bribing people. They can't find out until we get the signatures. It would definitely hurt our cause. I mean it would be catastrophic."

"Okay, Simon. I get it."

"And just so you know, if they do find out, Bill told me it's illegal for them to talk about it or threaten people or offer bribes or any shit like that. So keep your eyes and ears open."

Pots clang and a highpitched voice hollers, "Simon, get off the phone. I have to make a call."

"Listen, I gotta go, but keep working on those signatures. And remember, trust no one."

"Okay, Simon. Bye."

By Friday I sign up four deli ladies and Simon signs up all six stock boys, four cashiers, the butcher and the butcher's assistant. I walk into work on Tuesday and see Katrina and Frank talking near the reduced produce rack. Frank nudges Katrina and she stops talking. I walk into the backroom. The punch clock reads 3:59. Justin winds elastics around bunches of romaine lettuce. He looks up and runs to me still holding a romaine lettuce.

"Hey Rosa, you better hurry up and punch in."

"Why?"

"Simon got fired this morning. He was two minutes late and they fired him. Can you believe it? Two minutes. I'm serious. He was only late two minutes."

Mike and Darryl walk into the backroom. Justin pretends to get more elastics. I punch in, put on my apron and head toward the bakery.

Frank picks at a chocolate chip muffin in the bakery. I walk to the deli cooler to get a bucket of potato salad. Frank walks to the cooler and holds the door open for me. I move a buggy full of beef jerky, schnitzel and salami to get to the stack of buckets. To reach the top bucket, I stand on a box of bottled horseradish. A centimetre of water sits on the lid of the top bucket. I tug on the bucket handle. Water spills as I lower the bucket to the cooler floor. Frank leans on the cooler door.

"You know nothing is going to change with a union. They'll be taking at least an extra dollar off each pay cheque as a service charge."

I drag the bucket out of the cooler and across the floor to the counter. I bend my knees and try to lift it onto the counter, but the bucket slips and falls. Frank grabs the bucket and swings it onto the work counter. Wioletta and Edyta walk by on their way to the deli cooler.

Frank steps in front of Wiloetta and Edyta. "If you guys think you're getting benefits, you're not."

Wioletta and Edyta keep walking. I scoop potato salad into plastic containers.

A Heater and a Fan

"Look, I'm not allowed to be talking about it, but look at what happened to Simon. Where did it get him? A place in line at the unemployment centre, that's where. Trust me, a union won't change anything."

Mike struts into the bakery and stares at the display counter. Green letters spell CAW UNION on five white pencils that Helena set on the counter that morning. Mike picks up a pencil, pinches each end between a thumb and index finger and holds it in front of his face. He glares at me and Frank, then he glares at the deli ladies. He snaps the pencil and places it on the counter. He snaps the other four pencils, two at a time and drops them in the garbage.

The next day a sign above the punch clock reads:

STAFF MEETING LUNCHROOM 8:00 P.M.

Last year, Frank asked Mike to get us a lunchroom. Mike set up a brown table with steel legs and three brown, orange and yellow flowered vinyl kitchen chairs in the upstairs stock room. Two entrances access the upstairs stockroom: a wooden ladder near the milk cooler, or stairs from outside. Two days ago, Mike added an olive green refrigerator, four more chairs, a microwave, a couple of coat hooks and three lockers to the upstairs stockroom.

I climb the wooden ladder and squeeze past boxes of Kraft Salad Dressing and Rice-a-Roni. Darryl stands up. "All of yous help yourselves to pizza and pop. Wine and beer's in the fridge." Frank holds a beer and sits behind Darryl on a box of canned apple juice. The full-time cashiers sit at the table, the deli ladies sit on milk crates near the table and the part-timers sit on the floor.

After everyone settles, Darryl clears his throat. "Listen, yous guys. I thought it would be a good idear to have a meetin' and talk about what wees don't likes about this place. Thataway we can decide for ourselves if wees want a union, without these union guys coming in here and telling us what's good for us. Now Mike and Joanna got nuttin' to do with it—they're not here—so says whatever you guys gots on your mind."

Katrina shuffles paper and picks up a pen. Darryl points to Katrina. "Katrina here is goin' to write out what we says. Wees can pass it on to Joanna and Mike and see what they can do. So just raise your hands and start."

Edyta raises her hand.

"Go ahead. What's your name again?"

"Edyta."

"Got that Katrina?"

Katrina nods.

"My English no so good," Edyta says, "but I tell, uh, I told Rujia," she points to me, "to talk for me. For us. She knows." Edyta smiles at me. So do Wioletta and Ewa.

Darryl turns to me. "All right then, Rosa. Let's hear it."

I look up and see Katrina scribble.

"Well, first of all, people in the deli never get breaks." I clear my throat. "Mike and Joanna say that it's because the deli isn't busy all the time, so the deli workers can sit when it's not busy." I swallow and feel my face flush. "This just isn't the case. The deli is always busy—I mean there's always something to do, even if there are no customers. The deli workers should get scheduled breaks and lunches. I also think their breaks should be paid."

I lick my lips and wipe my forehead with the palm of my hand.

Darryl interrupts. "All right, Katrina did yous get that? Scheduled breaks and paid lunches?"

Katrina nods.

"Anyone else?"

I raise my hand.

"Rosie. Yous got more?"

"Yes. I wasn't done."

Darryl motions with his hand for me to continue, but Edyta waves her hand in front of me.

"Is okay, Rujia, I talk. You red like pepper."

Everyone laughs.

"We in deli work long time here. We work very hard. I here five years, Wioletta here eight years and Ewa three years—and still nothing. No money. We have family. Need more money. We work hard."

Someone yells, "We all do." Everyone complains to the person next to them.

Kelly raises her hand.

"Yous guys, yous guys calm down," Darryl cries out. "Little Kelly's got her hand up."

Kelly glances at the other part-time cashiers seated beside her on the floor. "It's just like, sometimes, like Mike is really mean and yells at us for no reason."

The other part-timers nod.

"It's just like, he doesn't have to be so mean. We like, don't even do anything wrong and he yells at us. Like last week, he made Annie cry. I was there and like she didn't even do anything wrong."

Darryl nods and winks. "Sweetie, I agree with you one hundred percent. Mike's got a bad temper. Katrina, you got that down?"

Katrina nods.

Nelson raises his hand. Darryl points to him. "Yup, Nelson, go ahead."

Nelson complains about how cold it is in the backroom in winter and requests a heater. Ruby complains about how hot it is in the bakery in the summer and requests a fan. Someone says "benefits" and "health plan" and the room buzzes. Nelson says "raises" and the room hums with "Ya" and "Damn right."

Frank clears his throat.

Darryl glances at him. "Calm down yous guys. Frank's goin' to git Mike and Joanna now and let's see what they can do for us."

Frank sits on the box of canned apple juice and does not move. A door opens at the back of the lunchroom and Mike and Joanna enter the room. No one speaks. Mike stands beside Frank. Joanna walks to the fridge to pour a glass of wine.

Mike scans the room. "Hey everybody, you like my new haircut?" He turns his head from side and side. Some people laugh. Joanna crosses the room and joins Mike.

"Okay," Mike says, "well you all know some people here think they would be better off with a union. Joanna and I don't think so. We are reasonable and fair and I think we can solve these problems without getting outside people involved." He scans the room again and nods at Katrina. "So let's hear these complaints."

Katrina lists our complaints and Mike responds.

"One: paid breaks and scheduled lunches," reads Katrina.

"Scheduling lunches is your department manager's duty," says Mike. "We allow the managers the freedom to regulate, so talk to them. As for paid breaks, it would be impossible to regulate without punching out. Continue punching out for breaks so people don't go over fifteen minutes, but we won't take it off your cheque."

People nod.

"Two: raises."

"I knew this would come up. You'll all get raises. I will talk to department managers about who deserves what. It might take a while to sort out, but I guarantee you will all get raises."

More people nod.

A Heater and a Fan

"Three: health plan and benefits."

Joanna steps forward. "We don't even have benefits or a health plan for ourselves, so that should go to show you. I mean we just can't afford it. We're a small business, not like these big chains. We just don't have the money for it."

Katrina lists more complaints. Mike denies his bad temper and kisses Joyce on the cheek. Joanna promises to buy Nelson a heater and Ruby a fan. Mike offers more pizza, beer, pop and wine. Mike and Joanna sling their arms around my shoulders and say how much they appreciate my hard work. Joanna hugs Ruby, Kelley, Kevin and Michelle. She gives each deli worker a can of apple juice to take home.

Mike apologizes to Annie and explains that on that particular day he remembers being in a bad mood. A lot of the full-timers leave. Katrina, Michelle, Joyce, Darryl, Frank and some of the part-timers finish the pizza. Others open another beer and some stay after the pizza and beer to smoke pot.

The next day Michelle, has stitches on her forehead. She fell off her bike riding home after the staff meeting. Darryl and Frank found her lying in the parking lot with one shoe on. Joyce found Michelle's other shoe in the fridge. Michelle pukes outside the bakery door as Helena, the bakery manager, marches in.

"I see you had a big party yesterday." Helena rolls her eyes and turns to me. "Zo, vut happened maan? Is dere a union or not?"

"The union reps are comin' in next Tuesday and the vote's next Friday."

Michelle gags. Her vomit hits the pavement.

"Vy doesn't she go to the vashroom? Vut's de matter vith her?"

I say nothing. A lineup blocks the washroom this morning. Joyce carries a paper bag in her back pocket, just in case. Darryl didn't make it to the washroom and puked in a half-empty bucket of coleslaw.

Michelle plods into the bakery with her hands on her forehead. "Maybe I should go on workers' comp." She laughs and leans against the counter.

Helena throws her an apron.

"Vell, union or no union, you have to verk. So get to verk or go home."

On Tuesday, I climb the ladder to the lunchroom to meet the union rep. Kelly talks and Michelle and Annie huddle around her.

"You're not going to believe it. Like, you know Mike. Like, yesterday he came up to me and said if we vote the union in, he's like going to close the store in the winter and only like open in the summer. So we'll all like be out of jobs for like four, five months."

Michelle covers her mouth with her hand. "Oh my God, Kel. Do you think he can do that? Oh my God. Where am I gonna get the money for our ski trip this winter? This sucks."

Annie rests her hand on her hip. "You guys, I don't think he can do that."

They peer up and huddle closer in their circle. Edyta, Wioletta and Ewa sit on milk crates.

Edyta yells, "Rujia, what about this scab? I hear Katrina say if we vote in they put this scab person to do our job. Is true, Rujia?"

"They're just trying to scare you. They—"

The union rep walks in and Edyta hushes me.

"Hello everybody. I'm your union rep. My name's Bill. How you all doing today?"

A Heater and a Fan

Michelle, Annie and Kelly sit on the floor. The full-timers stare at Bill. Wioletta, Ewa and Edyta stare at me. Bill hands out the blue, white and green pamphlets and thumb-tacks a white Bristol board to the wall. Three words written in capital letters read:

ENVIRONMENT, BENEFITS AND WAGES

"Alrighty. Well if everyone's settled down, we can get started. Now, first things first. I'm here to help you. So if you have any questions or comments please raise your hand. Now let's get down to business. I guar-en-tee you better wages. I guar-en-tee you'll get benefits and I guar-en-tee your work environment will improve. Who here would like to improve their work environment?"

Darryl sits on a box with his back to Bill. "What's good about improvin' the work environment," Darryl says, "if they don't let us through the door 'cause theys got scabs doin' our work?"

Wioletta and Ewa whisper. Kelly and Annie murmur to Michelle and Edyta glances at me. Katrina drops two spoons of sugar into her coffee and stirs.

"Now hold on folks, hold on." Bill nods and paces across the front of the room. "No one said anything about scabs. We are here to work out a collective agreement."

Darryl turns to face Bill. "Well can yous guar-en-tee we won't be replaced by scabs?"

Darryl and Katrina laugh and the stock boys snicker.

"Now hold on folks. I know where you're coming from. I know, my father worked in a factory all his life and let me tell you what I know. I know that my father was definitely one hundred percent better off when that factory got a union. Now, who here doesn't want to be better off?" Bill opens his hands toward us. "Better wages and a better work environment can do nothing but improve your work experience. Am I right?"

Darryl turns his back to Bill again. Bill reads the pamphlets to us and points to the words on the white Bristol board. Bill points to us, "I guarantee you a brighter future and an improved work experience. Do the right thing on Friday and vote yes." Most of the part-timers leave. The full-timers chatter around the table.

"Rujia, what this man say? I understand nothing. What is guarantee and this?" Edyta holds out the pamphlets. "This is useless to me, all in English. Rujia, what you think? Good or no good union?"

"It's good, Edyta."

"But what about this scab? And other girl say they close store."

"They're just trying to scare you."

"Yes. This I understand." Edyta sighs. "But you know Rujia sometimes I think is same—union, no union. Maybe different but just same. You know?"

Mike and Frank saunter into the lunchroom. Frank holds an order sheet and leans on a box near the full-time cashiers sitting at the table. Mike points at boxes and stares at Edyta, Wioletta, Ewa and me. Mike walks toward us; we walk toward the ladder.

Mike, Joanna and Bill hold the vote on Friday in the lunchroom. Mike and Joanna sit in chairs across from the voting table. I file into the room with the other employees. As I sit down to place my vote I feel Mike and Joanna's eyes follow my hand as I check the yes box. I rush out of the lunchroom and rub my wet palms on my jeans.

At four o'clock, Mike posts a piece of paper above the punch clock. The results show 83% voted no; 17% voted yes.

A Ballerina and a Nurse

I walk into the bakery and drop my school bag on the floor. I bend down to tie up my ten-hole Docs, now cracked in the creases. I bought them four years ago, when I first started working at Tipper's Fruit Market. Glancing up, I see two hairy legs in beige pantyhose and ratty runners. A piece of salami skin dangles from one of the shoelaces. I stand up.

"Rujia, I thought everyone suppose to get raise. That is what Mike say. No union and we get raise."

I stare at Edyta.

"Nothing Rujia. Five years I work and nothing, still seven dollars an hour. Wioletta, Ewa, them too—nothing."

Edyta fishes for the handkerchief she wedges in the waistband of her skirt and wipes her face.

"Is terrible. Awful. I hear this Darryl and Katrina and cashiers, they get raise and us, Rujia, nothing. Nothing. Rujia, what can we do?"

"How about Antoinetta?" I slip my apron over my head. "Did you talk to her?"

"Yes, but what can she do?" Edyta blows her nose and shakes her head. "Nothing, Rujia. Nothing."

"I heard Mike gave raises based on manager's recommendations. That's what I heard they did up at cash. Talk to Antoinetta. She can talk to Mike."

Edyta shakes her head. "Antoinetta, she more scared than us. Like this." She holds out her hands and makes them tremble.

"She no say nothing. Ah." Edyta wipes her tears. "I better off dead, at least my feet could rest." She looks down and leans on the outer edges of her shoes. A hole underneath the big toe gapes in the sole of each shoe. I remember when those white running shoes gleamed. On Edyta's first day of work in the deli department, I introduced myself.

"Hey there. Hello. Are you new? My name is Rosa."

"Ah, Rujia." The woman said smiling. "Me, Edyta." She pointed to herself.

"I work in the bakery," I said. "When it's not busy I help out in the deli. Any cheese for me to pack?"

"Ah. Ya. I ask Wioletta." Edyta turned to where Wioletta sliced turkey breast at the slicer. Grey roots peeked through Wioletta's fuzzy light brown hair. Her pink jogging pants stretched tight across her stomach and backside. Pink lipstick frosted her lips and turquoise eyeshadow smeared her eyelids.

"Cheese, ah, you need outside?" Edyta pointed to the deli counter.

"Ya, feta." Wioletta glanced at me. "Rujia knows."

Edyta walked with me to the deli fridge, straightening her brown, corduroy skirt and brushing off a strand of cooked ham. Her runners looked bright white and smooth.

"New shoes?" I said.

A Ballerina and a Nurse

"Ya. Friday I wore other shoes and—" She hissed through her teeth. "Ay, my feet."

We counted to three, lifted the bucket of feta cheese into a miniature shopping cart and wheeled it to the vacuum machine station. I lifted a block of feta cheese out of the water, placed it on the counter and cut it into chunks.

"Rujia, you know in Poland, I use to wear shoes like these too. Ya, in hospital. Ya, in Poland I was nurse."

I stopped cutting. "What are you doing here? Is this to hold you over until you find a job as a nurse?"

Edyta shook her head. "No. In Canada, Edyta no nurse. No English, no nurse."

"You can learn English. They have adult courses. You can take night school."

Edyta gazed at the feta. "First make money for my children and husband to come to Canada. Then learn English."

She bowed her head and smiled. I smiled back and dropped the feta in bags. The feta cheese crumbled as I picked it up.

"I hate packing feta cheese."

Edyta giggled and covered her mouth with her hand.

"What's so funny?"

"Wioletta is number one in packing feta. You ever see her do the feta?"

"Now that you mention it, she never makes half the mess I make."

"Secret." Edyta moved her head closer and glanced up at me. "Grace."

"Huh?"

"Wioletta has grace. Balance. In Poland, ballerina."

"You're kidding me."

Edyta snatched a piece of feta. "Wioletta dances with the feta." Edyta slipped the piece of feta in the plastic bag. "See. Precision, Rujia. Grace."

I laughed and the feta in my hand crumbled.

Wioletta approached us. "Edyta," she said. "Busy. Come serve."

"*Dobra.*" Edyta washed her hands and helped Wioletta serve the customers.

Joanna and Mike strode down the aisle to the deli counter. Mike held a bun and waved it at Antoinetta. Antoinetta stopped serving her customer, cut two slices of roast beef and a slice of Provolone cheese and slid the slices into the bun.

Joanna hung her arm around Edyta, shook her shoulder and in a loud voice said, "How are you today?" then laughed and walked toward me without waiting for a reply.

Edyta gave none.

"If my kids were here they'd say, 'Oooohhh, you're cutting cheese.'" Joanna laughed, again.

Mike looked at me and bit into his sandwich. I cut and packed feta cheese. I watched the vacuum-pack machine suck the air out of the small, plastic bags.

Edyta groans and slowly rolls her feet in, so her soles rest flat on the floor.

"Is terrible, Rujia. Awful. I hate this place. And for what?" She sticks out her index finger. "My daughter don't want to go to college." She sticks out her index and middle finger. "My son miss his friends. Miserable. And my husband, phu—" She waves her hand in the air. "Cannot find job."

Edyta sobs.

A Ballerina and a Nurse

Wioletta walks toward us. "Edyta, no cry. Change nothing." Wioletta's eyes well up. Her one hand carries a Genoa salami. The other clenches into a fist. A tear falls. She turns away, resting her hand on Edyta's shoulder.

They walk away leaning into the space between them.

The ballerina and the nurse wipe their tears and peel the skin off a Genoa salami.

Mike and Joanna walk to the deli counter. Mike hands Antoinetta a bun. Antoinetta cuts the roast beef. Wioletta cuts the Provolone cheese. Joanna hangs her arm around Edyta, shakes her shoulder and in a loud voice says, "And how are you today?"

Kwai Li

KWAI LI, born in India, to Hakka parents who emigrated from China in the 1920s, grew up in the Chinatown of Calcutta. Li immigrated to Canada in 1972, became a member of the Certified General Accountants of Ontario and now works part-time in accounting while studying Religion and Professional Writing at the University of Toronto. Li received a Canada Council writing grant in 1998.

Farewell, Calcutta

On a humid evening in August of 1972, my brother Swallow and I stood on the busy sidewalk of Chowringhee Avenue. A man elbowed me when he rushed past. Another man pushed me. I moved closer to Swallow.

Fluorescent lights from store windows reflected onto the faces of people around us.

Couples lingered at the shop windows. Women looked at saris, jewellery, sewing machines and gas stoves, and men admired cameras, posters of Bollywood actresses and spotlit cars in showrooms. Giggling girls dodged through crowds. Men loitered by the cold-drink stand and eyed the girls. Women, followed by servants, swept by with bulging shopping bags.

Cars, motorcycles, trams and buses crawled along the street. Drivers honked and shouted. Black clouds of exhaust wafted across the sidewalk.

Across Chowringhee Avenue, the crowds grew even denser at the Maidan, a sprawling parade ground used by the British in colonial days. In crowded Calcutta, the Maidan is the only piece of land empty of buildings.

At the edge of the Maidan, near the Hoogly River, squatters lived in a shantytown, sometimes eight to a shack—shacks not big enough for four people to lie down in at the same time. Shantytown dwellers bathed and relieved themselves in or near the river, and drank and cooked with Hoogly water. Refugees from Bangladesh, most had lost their homes during the War of Independence in December of 1971.

Lucky refugees worked as coolies and sweepers. Others spent their days going through garbage dumps. They gathered clothes, cardboard, metal, bottles and newspapers and sold them to recyclers for pennies a kilo. Many begged and stole. Artistic ones painted sores on their bodies and pretended to be blind, sick or crippled. Desperate ones sold sex to coolies and sweepers.

On the sidewalk of Chowringhee Avenue, dirty beggars sat against the wall outside The Grand Hotel. Their dirty grey forms marred the gold-trimmed, freshly-painted white wall of The Grand Hotel. Two doormen in white uniforms, red belts and red and white turbans stood inside the wrought-iron gate in front of the hotel.

A blond couple strolled towards the gate.

Beggars swarmed the couple, hands outstretched. "*Sahib and memsahib, baksheesh, baksheesh.*"

One woman in a tattered sari suckled a baby at her breast. The woman pointed at the baby and touched the female tourist on her arm.

"Go away. Shoo." The tourist flapped her hands.

The doormen opened the gate, surged out and slashed the air with their truncheons. The beggars fell back.

The tourists walked into the courtyard where subdued lights reflected off shiny brass fittings, where crystal chandeliers chimed in the air-conditioned breeze, where Ming vases sat on Chippendale tables and where the concierge quoted hotel charges in US dollars.

Across the road on the Maidan the Ochterlony Monument glowed, lit by a string of lights spiralling up the column. Under a canopy on a raised platform at the foot of the Monument, a man shouted into a mike about the government.

I raised my arms above my head, stood on tiptoe and laughed. "I am leaving for Canada tomorrow. I can't wait."

Swallow tapped me on the shoulder. "Patience, baby sister. You will be in Canada soon enough."

I stuck out my tongue at him. "You are going to miss me. Who are you going to scold when I am not here to act crazy?"

Swallow snorted.

I laughed.

We turned and walked towards New Market.

My parents had nine children. Swallow was the sixth and I was the ninth. My parents immigrated to Calcutta in the 1920s from Moiyan, in Southern China. My eldest sister, Chao, was born in 1927 and my second sister, Moi, in 1929. Father took them back to China in the early 1930s to visit our grandparents. Father came back to Calcutta alone. Grandmother told father to leave the children behind, so that he would not forget to send money back.

In 1948, Chairman Mao took over most of China. Father rushed back to China to rescue his daughters. Chao had married and had two children. My grandmother chose her husband.

The family story says two young women met my father's boat. My sisters had joined the Red Guards. They told Father that they wanted to stay and be part of the new China. "Please leave, Father, or we will be forced to detain you," Moi said.

Father took the first boat leaving for Hong Kong and then another boat back to Calcutta. He did not meet his grandchildren.

Moi had nine children in all, three of them older than me. Chao had six. Most of them stayed in the village and farmed.

Father found himself much poorer with Chairman Mao's takeover of China. He had invested his life savings on Kuomintang bonds. The bonds became worthless. We wallpapered one wall of our living area behind the Calcutta shoe-shop with the Kuomintang bonds.

My parents' eldest son, Panda, was born in 1934. When Panda was eight years old, my mother chose a wife for him. The Chinese in Calcutta often selected a wife for their young son. The parents then adopted the chosen baby girl and raised her with their son.

The Wongs lived across the street from our shoe shop on Bentinck Street. Mr. and Mrs. Wong had five daughters and two sons. Mother often visited Mrs. Wong. They sat outside the Wong shop and chatted.

During one of her visits, my mother joked with Mrs. Wong, "One of your daughters should be my daughter-in-law."

Mrs. Wong said, "Why not? Pick one. Which of my daughters would you like?"

The five Wong daughters sat in a row, fanning themselves. They giggled when Mother walked over to where they sat. Mother looked at each girl and murmured. "I would like my grandchildren to have nice noses. I want them to have bridges between their eyes. Not flat like mine. Your daughters have nice, fair skin. Good, good. My grandchildren will be fair also." She examined the five noses again and pointed to the third daughter, "I want her."

Mrs. Wong nodded. "She is yours. I will speak to my husband." My mother and Mrs. Wong went to the Buddhist temple. The monk checked the Chinese almanac for an auspicious date. A month later, the six-year-old Miss Wong moved across the street with her belongings and became a part of the Li family. When Panda reached twenty-one, he married my sister-in-law.

I was born to Mother in her late forties. My two-year-old sister, Jade, had tuberculosis. My mother had a rough time looking after a sick child and a newborn baby. When I was a week old, my parents found a couple to adopt me. They had the same last name, "Li." When I learned to talk, I called my natural parents "Father Sak" and "Mother Sak." Sak was my father's name. I called my adoptive parents "Father" and "Mother."

Mother Sak saw me every week. She brought baby food, clothes and diapers. She also promised to pay for my education when I went to school.

As I grew, my siblings dreaded my visits. Mother Sak told her other children to let me play with their toys. I had temper tantrums if my siblings refused to lend me their toys. Jade hid her dolls whenever she heard me coming. Jade, a quiet figure, sat in a reclining chair, her teeth red with the blood she coughed up. Jade died when she was six.

Father Sak died of a heart-attack two years later.

For our weekly dinners, Mother Sak and my sister-in-law prepared food on two coal-burning stoves. Mother Sak then took portions of each dish and set up a small, low table in the shop. We sat on stools and ate our meal, just Mother Sak and me. She said that my elder siblings were too noisy. In the living quarters behind the shop, my four brothers, my sister and my sister-in-law ate at a large, round table. Mother Sak ate in silence. I chattered. She told me that I talked too much, just like Father Sak.

Mother always asked me about my visit with Mother Sak. "What did Mother Sak ask you?"

"Nothing, Mother. She was very quiet."

"What did you talk about?"

"I told her about the shrimp dish you made last week. I loved it. I told her about my school. I told her that I hated English in school. It is a difficult language to learn. Mother, when I graduate from Chienko, could I go to the university in Taiwan? Mr. Ma, the principal, told me I could get a scholarship."

"I don't know. We'll talk about it in a few years' time."

My adoptive parents had no children of their own. They adopted a baby boy, Nan, and left him with an uncle in China. In Calcutta, Father and Mother also adopted a five-year-old girl, Autumn, in 1943, to be the wife of Nan. Two years after my adoption, Mother adopted one-year-old Fu. Fu's Indian mother died at Fu's birth. Fu's Chinese father planned to return to China. Fearing his family in China would not accept a dark-skinned child, he gave up Fu for adoption.

When I learned to walk, Father took me walking on the street to show me off. Chattawalla Gully, the small road that ran off Sun Yat Sen Street, the main street of Chinatown, had two tea stalls. Every evening, the tea-stall owners raked out their coal-burning stoves and left the ashes in the middle of the road. One evening, Father did not notice that I left my shoes home. I stepped on a pile of hot ashes.

When Father died six months later, Mother told me that he died of fright at seeing the melon-sized blisters on the soles of my feet. After Father's death, Mother grew bean sprouts to sell to Chinese restaurants. She also made salted vegetables for the market. My sister-in-law Autumn looked after Fu and me.

When I was four years old, a neighbour told Father Sak and Mother Sak that Mother ill-treated me. Mother took me to the shoe shop on Bentinck Street. She undressed me and asked Mother Sak to look for bruises on my body. It was a business day and a crowd gathered. Mother Sak soothed Mother and told her that she did not believe Mother could ill-treat anyone, especially me.

No one thought to look under my hair. Autumn often hit Fu and me on the head. When I was five, I broke a china spoon as I washed dinner dishes. Autumn tied my wrists behind me and locked me in a dark room. I carried a lump, sometimes three, on my head until I was eleven. When Autumn had her first child, I told her that I would beat up her son if she ever hit me again.

Nan, my adoptive brother, arrived in Calcutta in 1959. He married Autumn a month after his arrival. They had four sons and one daughter. Their eldest son died of cholera at six. Chien, a gentle child, like a soft breeze, slipped past me before I could touch him.

After the birth of her third son, Autumn joined a mahjong group. Nan hated his wife's gambling habit. One day Autumn lost the rent money. Nan and Autumn fought. I took the children to the third-floor terrace and told them stories.

I spent seven years in a Chinese medium school. Mother felt proud. I competed for the first place in class every year. Mother showed my report cards to her friends when she visited them. She told me I disappointed her whenever I came in second.

I read to escape from Autumn. I read children's stories, Kung Fu novels, romances, mythologies and any other books I could find. I read the three volumes of Father's *Three Kingdoms* in classical Chinese. Fu was not as lucky. He did not have another family in Calcutta as I did on Bentinck Street. He did not enjoy reading and he did badly in school. Fu left home at age fourteen and we heard nothing from him for six years.

Mother Sak had a stroke when I was twelve. My twenty-year-old sister, Lady, quit school and looked after her. Mother Sak could not speak or do anything for herself. I sat beside her. She lay on her back, her eyes closed. A tear crept from under her left eyelid and crawled down the side of her face. I touched her hand. She opened her eyes and looked at me. We cried.

Mother Sak died eighteen months later. I overheard two neighbours talking. They said that I was an unnatural child because I did not weep at Mother Sak's funeral.

I visited my siblings on Bentinck Street once a week after Mother Sak's death. I told Mother I needed help with my school work.

When I finished my schooling in Chienko Chinese School, I wanted to apply for a scholarship and study in Taiwan. Mother refused and asked my brother Panda to enrol me in an English medium school.

Since the shoe shop was faltering, Panda put me in the cheapest school he could find: Sacred Heart Girls' School. Miss David, a stern woman in her fifties with frosty grey hair and pale, cold eyes, ran Sacred Heart.

Miss David, a devout Catholic, believed in discipline. She set up large wooden tables in all the rooms of her house. The Class One students studied in her large bedroom. Miss David's dresser and bed crowded against one wall, her tall closet against the opposite wall, to make space for the four tables in the middle of her room. Class Two through Seven students sat on benches, facing each other over the six scarred wooden tables in Miss David's tennis court-sized living room. The students sat one class, eight to fifteen students, to each table.

Miss David had three teachers to help her. The teachers presided at the head of the tables. The students feared Miss David. So did the teachers. I started at Sacred Heart Girls' School in Class Three.

Every morning, we knelt on the floor and started school with "Hail Mary" and "The Lord's Prayer," then we sat at the table for an hour of catechism and Bible instruction. We recited passages from the Bible. Miss David walked between the tables, her hands behind her back. She tapped a cane against her calves as she walked.

Miss David's living room had no outside window. Four sixty-watt light bulbs swung in the breeze of the ceiling fans. Shadows glided as the lights swung. The voices of seventy students echoed off high ceilings.

Anella sat beside me. At fifteen, Anella had thick, blue-black hair, dark, sad eyes and huge breasts. After the morning prayers, the students filed past Miss David to get to their seats. Miss David looked each student over. She told us that we should not wear brassieres. "Brassieres are sinful. They push your breasts up and display your busts. The Bible says that girls should be modest. Pushing your breasts up is not modest."

Miss David stared hard at Anella on the first day of school and told the whole school a story about sinful girls who wore bras and burned in hell. From that day on, Miss David singled out Anella for punishment. Anella slouched, but her breasts still stood out.

Anella's voice wavered when Miss David passed behind her. One day, Miss David stopped and asked Anella to read a paragraph from page twenty of the Old Testament. The room grew quiet. Anella stammered and stumbled and burst into tears. "Alright, Anella, you have not been reading the Old Testament at home, have you?"

Anella sobbed.

Miss David slammed the cane on the table. Everyone jumped.

"Answer me, Anella! Have you been reading?"

Anella whispered, "No, Miss."

Miss David shouted, "Have I not told you to study the Bible at home?"

Anella spoke into her handkerchief, "Yes, Miss."

Whack! Miss David caned the table again. "Speak up, Anella."

Anella jumped. She lowered her handkerchief, closed her eyes and lifted her head. Tears dribbled down her face and fell onto the blouse where her sinful breasts jutted. "Yes, Miss."

"Hold out your hand."

Miss David caned Anella five times, three times on her left palm and twice on her right. Anella had trouble writing for three days.

When I graduated from Chienko Chinese School, I barely knew my English alphabet. For the first six months in Sacred Heart, I spent my evenings memorizing passages for the next day. My sister Lady helped me with my reading. I wrote Chinese transliterations beside the English words I had trouble with. In spite of Miss David, I enjoyed reading the Old Testament with its murders, rapes, incest, political and family intrigues, wars and blood sacrifices.

Miss David rented students books published in the 1920s, and yellowed with age. Miss David regarded herself as an Englishwoman, despite her dark skin. Miss David and the teachers taught English history and English geography. They taught nothing about India.

I stayed at Sacred Heart for three long years, until Dalhousie Girls' School accepted me. Someone in the United States, someone known as "the Sponsor," paid my school fees. Although the sponsor paid all the fees, my parents had to pay a monthly fee as well.

Every six months, two administrators from the Dalhousie Charitable Foundation came to the school. They handed a letter to each of the sponsored students (about one hundred of us) and we copied the letter exactly. The letter read:

> *Dear Sponsor,*
> *Thank you for the ten/fifteen/twenty dollars you sent me. I used it to buy a shawl for my mother and some books for myself. I loved the dresses you sent. They fitted me perfectly.*
> *Once again, thank you very much for all you have done for me and God bless you.*

The sponsored students did not know the names and addresses of their sponsors, nor did they receive the money and the presents. The school expelled any student who refused to copy the letter.

Mrs. Joseph, the principal, was an Anglo-Indian—an Indian Christian who saw herself as English. She retired and "returned" to England during my second year at Dalhousie. Miss James, our music teacher, put together a concert for her retirement. We sang "Somewhere over the Rainbow." Mrs. Joseph returned to Calcutta a year later. She found England too cold and too wet.

Miss Chowdhuri became our principal. In her fifties, she weighed about two hundred and fifty pounds. Makeup caked her face and her small heavily khohled eyes stared out from puffy lids. Her cold stare reminded me of Miss David.

I enjoyed the three years I spent at Dalhousie. Unlike Sacred Heart, each class at Dalhousie had its own classroom. I studied English, literature, science, cooking, sewing and music, as well as Hindi and Bengali, which I did not study in Sacred Heart. I read Shakespeare and Orwell for the first time. I dissected a mouse for the first time. My classmate, Shamila, fainted when the mouse squealed and struggled. I did well in school. I made Mother proud when I won almost all the awards for the class.

A year after my graduation, I prepared to leave for Canada. The week before I left Calcutta, Mother took me to the Chinese cemetery. We offered three meats, three fruits and three cups of tea before the graves of Father, Father Sak and Mother Sak. I burned Chinese candles, incense and imitation money for the three of them. I bowed three times before their graves and asked for their protection and blessing.

Mother also donated money to Buddhist temples and asked the monk to chant prayers for my safe journey.

Swallow and I walked past the Paradise Cinema. The evening show had ended and the crowd flowed out. Sean Connery leered from the billboards. A shiny, almost naked woman covered in gold powder lay at his feet. Three half-naked women clutched his arms and shoulders. It was a rerun of *Goldfinger*. The cinema crowd walked slowly, reluctant to leave a world of beautiful women, handsome heroes and perfect villains.

We walked past a small park. Rabindranath Tagore stood on the pedestal and looked down on the refugees from Bangladesh who camped in the postage stamp-sized park. The grass had long ago been eaten by the refugees' goats. A rusty iron fence held clothes spread out to dry. The street gutters reeked of feces and urine. In the flickering light of the cooking fires, men smoked bilris, cheap hand-rolled cigarettes. Women rocked and sang to sleepy babies.

Farewell, Calcutta

We turned the corner and walked along Bentinck Street, away from the bright lights and loud music of the tourist district. A rickshaw-*wallah* (puller) clanged his hand-bell and a couple from the cinema haggled with the rickshaw-*wallah* and got onto the rickshaw. The rickshaw-*wallah* lit the oil lamp that hung under the seat. He picked up the shaft, ran down the empty street and disappeared around a bend in the road. On the sidewalk, shadowy figures spread out their pallets, lay down on the pavement and prepared for sleep. Soon the chattering dwindled into occasional coughs and footsteps.

Swallow touched me on the arm, "Let's go home."

I turned for home, for the last time, in Calcutta.

A Fish Who Invited Itself to Dinner

When I was ten years old, a prolonged monsoon rain fell steadily for three weeks and flooded Calcutta. The streets became waterways and rats, cats and dogs took refuge on half-submerged rickshaws, cars and buses.

We lived in the Chinatown of Tangra, a square mile of sprawling, one-storey buildings, leather tanneries, restaurants and shops owned by the Chinese. Tangra sits on reclaimed swampland, surrounded by ponds, fish farms, garbage dumps and open sewers.

My brother and I played around the fish ponds. We threw pieces of bread into the water and tried to catch the fish as they swam close to the bank to gobble the food.

The schools had closed. So had the markets. Mother searched for fresh meat and vegetables among the few vendors who got through the flood. Six inches of murky brown water sloshed over the floors of our apartment. Mother used bricks to elevate the furniture above the water.

As the canals and ponds overflowed, the roads became impassable. The Chinese got together at Mrs. Chiu's place to discuss evacuation plans. Before leaving for the meeting, Mother told my brother and me not to leave the rooms.

"You be a good elder sister and look after Fu," she said. "Don't let him get into trouble."

Fu and I made boats out of newspaper and fought battles under the table and chairs. After two hours, Fu and I grew tired and bored. We sat on the edge of the bed. Our bare feet stirred the water. We watched the last of our boats sink under the table. The week's washing hung on lines strung across the room and smelled of mildew.

"You think we can sneak out to the fish pond?" I asked. I thought of the fish farm about a ten-minute walk from our apartment.

"Where is the fish pond?"

The walkways between the ponds had flooded. One great pond spread outside our building, a pond steadily pock-marked by rain drops. From our window, I could see a dead cow in the pond. An abandoned rickshaw lay on its side, half submerged outside Mrs. Chiu's house. A dog cowered under the rickshaw's torn canvas covering.

We sat and listened to the rain hit the corrugated iron roof. I slapped at a mosquito buzzing by my left ear.

A dead mouse floated gently by and bumped against the base of one of the table legs.

"We should get rid of it," Fu said.

"You do it. I don't want to get my feet wet."

The mouse drifted away from the table and glided toward us.

"There is something moving under the table." Fu pulled his feet up.

"The mouse's big mama," I giggled.

Last year, a sewer rat bit Fu's toe while he slept. Mother took him to the doctor's for shots. After the shots, Fu feared the doctors as much as he feared the rats.

A Fish Who Invited Itself to Dinner

A silvery shape darted from under the table towards the mouse. The shape nibbled at a mouse leg.

"Fish!" we shouted.

I dove and collided with Fu. I splashed onto the floor, slid along the slime and banged my head against a chair.

We sat up and wiped gritty water from our faces. Fu pushed his hair back from his face. Bits of clay and pond weed and slime clung to his skin. We smelled of rotting vegetables, mildew and mould.

"Mother is going to kill us," I said as I wrung water from my hair.

"Let's kill the fish first."

"Yeah. Let's have it for dinner."

The carp was a foot long, probably an escapee from the fish farm.

I pointed at the dead mouse draped over Fu's big toe. "You'd better get rid of that first."

He yelped and shook his leg.

I reached over, picked the mouse up by its tail and laid it on a brick pile. We waited for the murky water to clear.

"There." Fu nodded towards the bed. "You go under the bed and chase the fish towards me."

I stood up. Water ran in brown rivulets off my shorts onto my legs.

The carp darted from under the bed. Fu pounced. He missed.

We chased the carp around the room and under the furniture. We splashed, we jumped, we stalked, but the fish eluded us.

One of the washing lines broke. Fu charged into my school uniform and tripped over a brick. He fell, taking a chair with him. One of Fu's school shirts floated above the sunken boats under the table. Shades of grey and slimy brown stained the once-white shirt.

Fu trapped the carp with one of Mother's blouses. He laughed as the bundle wriggled.

The door opened. "What...?" Mother looked around the room, her eyes widened. Fu and I looked at each other. Fu held the fish out to Mother and said, "Dinner."

Fu and I rewashed the clothes from the broken line, got rid of the waterlogged boats, and cleaned and dried the bed, the table and the chairs.

Mother prepared the carp in soya sauce and ginger, and we devoured it.

That night, we slept under a canopy of wet clothes. The mosquitoes whined, and the clothes dripped overhead.

The next day, the rain stopped and the water receded slowly. The smell of mildew, mould and rotting vegetables remained for a month after the monsoon.

The East Is Red

I sat on a low stool and built mud islands in a puddle left by the early morning monsoon rain. Sweat mixed with the mud caked on my left cheek. Mud smeared my pink dress. The wet, sticky mud felt cool as I dug from the sides of the puddle to build three islands in the middle. I added bridges between the islands with twigs and grass. A mosquito buzzed around my head. I swatted, adding a fresh smear to my face. I looked up and saw a girl, about my age, standing by the back doorway of the bookshop, her face wet.

"Why are you crying?" I asked.

"I am not crying. It's raindrops on my face."

"What are raindrops doing on your face?"

She looked at her feet.

I looked at my dress, stiffened and brown with mud and then at the girl's clean blouse and shorts. "Would you like to play Islands and Bridges with me, Raindrop?" I asked.

Raindrop later told me that she missed her mother, who had died two months before. Raindrop's father had owned a restaurant in Shillong, a hill station near the Indo-Chinese border. After her mother's death, Raindrop's father sold the restaurant, moved to Calcutta and opened a bookstore.

For the next four months, Raindrop and I spent many hours in the small, muddy courtyard. We dug puddles and sailed our paper boats. We chased chickens around the courtyard and tracked mud into our apartments. Soon the monsoon ended and the sky cleared and the weather cooled.

One warm February afternoon, a week before Chinese New Year, Raindrop and I sat on the windowsill of my family's apartment. The window overlooked the courtyard, where the mud puddles had dried into dusty hollows. The back doors and windows of a row of one-storey shops opened onto the courtyard. The shops had red-tiled, pagoda-like roofs. Bamboo matting peeked through gaps of missing tiles and the shop-owners complained of leaky roofs when it rained. The shops fronted onto Sun Yat Sen Street, the main street of Chinatown.

Three of the four shops belonged to the Chinese who lived and worked in them. Mrs. Liu sold salted peanuts. She boiled her peanuts in a large, metal pot over a coal stove. Mrs. Liu then drained the water from the peanuts, still in their shells, and spread them on round bamboo trays. Sometimes Raindrop and I helped her. Mrs. Liu climbed a rickety wooden ladder to place the trays on the roof. Red paper strips, tied to the handles of the trays, blew in the wind and scared the sparrows, pigeons and crows away from the peanuts.

Mr. Chen lived in the shop next to Mrs. Liu. He imported and sold Chinese groceries. Mr. Chen stored soya, black bean and other sauces in big-bellied, foot-high ceramic jars. Sometimes, when he ran out of storage space in the shop, he moved the jars to the courtyard. Under Mr. Chen's windows, Raindrop and I counted six large jars of sauces.

The East Is Red

The third shop belonged to Mr. Tai, Raindrop's father. When we didn't chase chickens, dig in the mud, or splash in the flooded courtyard, Raindrop and I went through the magazines and children's books in his Chinese-language bookstore. We pretended to read the magazines and books and made up stories from the pictures.

An Indian restaurant occupied the largest of the four shops. Phiroz, the restaurant owner, had covered his section of the courtyard with a corrugated iron roof. During the busy time, customers overflowed to the courtyard extension. I sometimes watched them sit cross-legged on the floor, their metal plates on their knees, chatting as they rolled rice into balls with their right hands, dipped the balls in curry and chutney, then lifted the rice balls and rolled them into their mouths.

Raindrop and I watched a pigeon chase a crow away from Mrs. Liu's peanut trays, then sit on the peanuts, spread its left wing and scratch its tail feathers with its foot. Now and then the pigeon pecked at the peanuts.

The restaurant's two cooks sat on coconut matting on the dirt floor in the courtyard and prepared food for the evening rush. The curry cook sat with his legs bent, his knees touching his ears. He chopped eggplants, onions, potatoes and tomatoes on a chopping board between his feet and threw the chopped pieces into a bowl in front of him. The chapati cook sat with a big, metal bowl and prepared dough for chapatis, an Indian flat bread. His knees spread lotus fashion and the soles of his feet gripped the bowl. His two hands kneaded and rolled the dough. He coughed and sneezed while he kneaded.

The curry cook said, "Ali is going back to the village soon."

The chapati cook paused in his kneading, "Ahchoo!"

"He is going to get married, you know," the curry cook said.

"Ah…" The chapati cook raised his left hand and covered his nose.

The curry cook reached for a potato. "His wife is quite old. Fourteen, I think."

"Choo!" The chapati cook wiped his nose with his forearm and resumed kneading.

Raindrop and I giggled at the smears of flour on the chapati cook's nose and cheeks. We sat on the windowsill and swung our legs.

Mrs. Liu came out with the ladder on her shoulder. She saw us and waved, "Hello, minnows. Want to help?"

"Yes, Aunty Liu."

We stood on either side of the ladder to steady it for Mrs. Liu while she climbed to reach the trays of peanuts.

Mrs. Liu removed all the trays from the roof. She asked Raindrop and me to guard the trays while she took them indoors, one at a time. When she had finished, Mrs. Liu rewarded us each with a handful of peanuts.

Mrs. Liu patted me on the head and said, "Tell your mother not to forget the mahjong tonight."

Mrs. Liu and Mother played mahjong with their friends almost every evening. The players held mahjong games in Mrs. Liu's shop, so that she could attend to customers between games.

"We are going over to Mrs. Liu's for dinner," said Mother later that evening.

I asked if Raindrop could come too.

"Yes. But ask Mr. Tai first."

Raindrop's father grunted when we asked him. He did not look up from his newspaper. Raindrop and I went with Mother to Mrs. Liu's.

The East Is Red

"I made cucumber salad and bought beef curry, curried rice and chapatis from Phiroz's," said Mrs. Liu. "His chapati cook is very good."

Raindrop and I looked at the chapatis on the table, then at each other. "Mother," I tugged at her hand. "Mother."

"How many people are playing tonight?" Mother asked Mrs. Liu.

"Mother, the chapati—" I whispered.

"Now, love, remember what I told you many times before? Don't interrupt me when I am talking." Mother frowned at me.

I let go of mother's hand and sat down at the table with Raindrop.

Raindrop and I ate only curried rice that night, while the others enjoyed the chapatis.

After dinner, Raindrop and I went to her father's shop. Mr. Tai and his friend Mr. Mo sat on the concrete seat outside the bookshop. Their cigarette smoke drifted into the shop and the living quarters. The bookshop, like the neighbouring shops, had a narrow shopfront, but a deep interior. Mr. Tai had strung a curtain between the shop and the living quarters. Raindrop and I lay on our stomachs on her bed with a magazine in front of us. It was the Chinese New Year edition of the *People's Monthly*.

"How can you say that the Communists are good for China?" said Mr. Mo.

Mr. Tai looked at his bookshelves. "Before Chairman Mao, the people in my village could not read or write. Chairman Mao opened the first school in my village. Now all the children can learn to read and write. What is better than reading and writing?"

"Ah, Bookworm, you know that you will be regarded as a capitalist pig in China? You have a shop; you own property. What is more important? You will get into trouble with the Indian Government." Mr. Mo shook his head.

"Look," said Mr. Tai, "I agreed with the Chinese Communist Government about China. Why should the Indian Government worry about what I think about China?"

"Chairman Mao's Red Army is only a few hundred miles from Calcutta. It's politics, Bookworm, politics." Mr. Mo coughed and spat in the gutter. He sighed and shook his head again.

I said to Raindrop, "I heard Mr. Chen argue about Mao and Chiang with his friends yesterday."

Raindrop turned the pages of the *People's Monthly*, stopped at a page and pointed, "This is Chairman Mao."

I put my head on Raindrop's shoulder and squinted. "Blackie looked like that when he stole a piece of beef from the cook," I said. Blackie was the resident dog at Phiroz's. Last week, when the cook sat in the courtyard chopping beef, Blackie snuck up, snatched and swallowed a piece before the cook could stop him. "But he looks nice. Chairman Mao, I mean."

"Of course he is nice. He is nicer than Chiang Kai Shek. Father said Chairman Mao is a good man." Raindrop pushed my head off her shoulder.

"My brother Panda said they are both wicked men," I said. "Lots and lots and lots of people died because Mao and Chiang fought and fought and fought."

"No. Lots and lots and lots of people died because Chiang Kai Shek is a wicked, wicked, wicked man," Raindrop shouted. "My father said so."

"My brother said they are both wicked and my brother knows everything," I shouted back.

"Children, what's the matter?" Mr. Tai walked in.

The East Is Red

Raindrop and I glared at each other. Mr. Tai looked at Chairman Mao's picture and sighed. "Little girls should not worry about such things." He closed the magazine and sat on the bed. "Would you like me to tell you a story?"

"Yes, please," we said. I lay on my side and hugged a pillow.

Mr. Tai thought for a moment. "Well, next week is Chinese New Year. When I was a little boy, I lived in a small village in Shantung. A month before the New Year, mother sent my brother and me to the market...."

We fell asleep before Mr. Tai finished his story.

The five Chinese language schools in Calcutta split into two factions: three schools supported Chiang Kai Shek, while the other two supported Mao Tse Tung. The two factions competed against each other in the Chinese New Year celebrations. On New Year's Eve, Lady, my fourteen-year old sister, took me to Shing-Fa, one of the schools. She had heard that Shing-Fa hired a good cook. My brothers went to Mai-Kwang, a supporter of Chiang.

Red flags flew from the front gate of Shing-Fa, from the rooftop and from bamboo poles in the playing field. Chairman Mao's foot-high picture, framed by yards of red cloth, smiled from a second floor window of the main building. Red refreshment tents swayed in the wind. Chinese lanterns hung between the tents. In front of the basketball net in the playing field, two ten-foot bamboo poles held up a large white canvas sheet that served as a screen for the evening movie, *The White Haired Girl*.

Five loudspeakers surrounded the school, one on the outside of the main building and the other four on trees around the playing field. The screen in front of the basketball net showed endless rows of men who marched and sang, "The East is Red...." and "Forward,

forward, forward...." The camera angle changed and showed crowds of children, all wearing red neckerchiefs. The girls wore red ribbons in their hair. The happy children smiled and waved red flags and threw flowers at the equally happy men who marched and sang.

Two girls in khaki uniforms and red neckerchiefs handed out small red flags at the front gate of the school.

Lady had arranged to meet her friends at the school. She found them at one of the refreshment tents. I pulled on Lady's hand, "Ah Chi (elder sister), I am hungry."

Lady told me to stay with Manny, one of her friends. She walked to the dumpling stand and came back with a plate of steamed dumplings. She gave me one. I looked around as I ate.

The Chinese packed the school grounds. Groups of teenage girls chatted and laughed. They glanced at the young men from the corners of their eyes. The young men stood near the girls, eyeing them and pretending not to notice their glances. At the base of the banyon tree, the only tree on the school compound, my neighbours Jade, Chung, Ma-lin and Fei sat on blankets with their mothers. Jade waved. I waved back. Chung, Ma-lin and Fei jumped up and ran around the tree. Nearby, Jade's father smoked cigarettes with his friends. They looked around and spoke to each other in loud voices.

The marching songs stopped and *The White Haired Girl* began. Lady and her friends grabbed more food. We sat down on the grass to watch the movie.

I sat beside Lady with a small plate of chickpeas, potatoes and cucumber with garam masala on my lap. I speared a piece of potato with a toothpick.

On the screen, the heroine, who still had black hair, walked toward the landlord, a fat man with tiny eyes, a big nose and crooked teeth.

The heroine and her family could not pay the rent and the landlord evicted them. She begged the landlord to let her dying parents stay in the house. The heroine knelt before the landlord and sang. The strings of a *bhi-pa* twanged in the background. Her parents pleaded. The landlord stroked his moustache and eyed the heroine.

The landlord said, "I will keep you for the back rent. Servants, hold this girl." Two servants grabbed the heroine.

The landlord pointed at the girl's parents, then at the door. "Throw them out." Drum beats roared as the servants dragged the parents out and slammed the door.

The landlord leered. "Now take her to the bedroom."

The heroine wailed, the chorus screeched, the music swelled and I fell asleep with my head on Lady's lap.

Lady shook me awake. "The movie is almost finished. Time to go home." On the screen, two years had passed. The landlord knelt before the heroine. The heroine's hair had turned white. Men in khaki uniforms and red arm bands stood behind her. Red stars glittered on their khaki hats. Guns glinted in their hands. The heroine held a large red flag with yellow stars. The wind whipped the flag and her hair flew out behind her. The landlord cried and begged her for mercy. The heroine sang, the men chorused and the landlord wailed.

Manny whispered, "Do you think her hair can really turn white overnight because she was, well, you know, by the landlord?"

Lady shrugged. "I don't know. There are always stories of people's hair turning white when something really bad happens to them."

The uniformed girls walked up and handed us leaflets with Chairman Mao's pictures on the front.

Our neighbour, Mr. Chen, walked up to Lady and told her to leave the school through the back door. "The Indian Secret Police are waiting outside," he whispered. "We think they record the names of those who attend this celebration."

Lady and her friends looked out the front door. Five men stood in the dark doorway opposite the school.

"Are they really the Secret Police?"

"They don't look like Secret Police."

"What do Secret Policemen look like?"

"Come on everyone, we'd better leave by the back door, just in case," Lady said.

Lady picked me up and hurried through the back door of the school.

A week later, Raindrop and I sat on the window sill with the latest *People's Monthly* open on my lap. Mother and Mrs. Liu stood with their backs to us. "The police arrested the Lo and the Ki brothers yesterday for disturbing the peace," Mother said to Mrs. Liu. "They had a fist fight in the marketplace."

"Why?" Mrs. Liu frowned. "I thought they were good friends."

"No." Mother shook her head. "It was the Communist and the Nationalist thing. It is getting out of hand. This is the third fight this week over stupid politics."

Mrs. Liu sighed. "There is going to be trouble. Big trouble. You know that the police came to Mr. Tai's. They asked him all sorts of questions."

"Oh. I didn't know that," Mother said. "When was that?"

"Two days ago. The police thought Mr. Tai spied for the Chinese Communists."

"Ahya. I told Mr. Tai not to speak out in favour of the Communists. He never listens."

Mother turned and saw us. She told us to go and read in the bookshop.

The East Is Red

A month after the Chinese New Year celebration, the Indian police came for Mr. Tai. That night, harsh voices in the courtyard woke me. I thought I heard Raindrop cry out. Mother came, patted me and said, "Go back to sleep. Everything is alright." I snuggled against Mother and went back to sleep.

In the morning, I ran to Mr. Tai's shop. Men in army uniforms ransacked the shop. The men overturned the bookshelves, dragged drawers out of the desk and pulled the beds apart. They threw books, clothing, pots and pans into large cartons and carried them to a truck parked outside.

Mother hurried over, picked me up and carried me back to our apartment.

"Mother, where is Raindrop? What are those men doing in Mr. Tai's shop?"

"Ssh. Mr. Tai and Raindrop have gone back to China. The police took them to the dock last night."

"But mother! Raindrop is my best friend. She can't go to China."

"Hush. She is gone. You will find a new friend. Lots of new friends. I promise."

I found a copy of the *People's Monthly* under a chair in the courtyard. Mother told me to throw it away or we might get into trouble with the police.

I hid the magazine under my bed.

Years later, I found the magazine in a shoebox. Chairman Mao's face, streaked with mould and mouse droppings, smiled up at me. I tore up the magazine and used it to start the coal fire for our evening meal.

Police Raid on Moonshine Pond

Christmas day of 1960 was cold. Mei Ling and I sat on a bench beside Tangra Road in Tangra. We leaned against the Chung Tannery wall with our feet on the bench, our skirts pulled over our toes and our chins on our knees. The wind whipped dust against the high, windowless walls on either side of the street. Along the street, tanneries rose dark and silent, their wide gates bolted shut from the inside.

A baby cried. A woman's voice murmured and the baby hushed.

Mei Ling and I hugged our legs against our chests and huddled together for warmth. The cold wind blew through my three layers of sweaters. The only street light on the block shone outside Mr. Liu's restaurant, a quarter of a mile from where we sat. Two dogs rooted in the garbage heap outside the restaurant.

Mei Ling shivered. "It is too quiet on the street. Where is everyone?"

"In bed, nice and warm," I said.

"Yeah. I wish Woody was here. He promised to get back."

Woody, Mei Ling's elder brother, had gone to Calcutta to see a special Christmas movie with his friends. Before he left, he promised his mother that he would be back by six o'clock. By nine o'clock,

Woody had not returned. Mother sent Mei Ling and me out onto Tangra Road to watch for the police.

Earlier that afternoon, Mother had asked me to bring some firewood into the shed by the Moonshine Pond.

I carried firewood from the courtyard into the shack and piled it beside four large bricks.

"You are a good girl," Mother said as she hurried out. She turned to me from the doorway, "Go and remind Mrs. Lee to put two half-bottles of Chinese moonshine in the goose's nest for the police."

The moonshiners always leave two bottles of moonshine for the police to find. Two months ago, when the police found no "hidden" moonshine, they broke everything in the shack.

"Mother." I ran after her. "Where are you going?"

"To the teashop. Go and see what Fu is doing." Mother waved and hurried down the footpath towards Mr. Chung's tannery, the only way out from our apartment and Moonshine Pond to Tangra Road.

The moonshiners paid a monthly fee to one of the policemen. When the police planned a raid, the police friend went to a teashop at the Tangra bus stop and left a message about the raid. The alcohol branch of the Tangra police also received regular cash presents from the moonshiners.

The police friend left no message.

"Maybe the police won't come tonight," Mother said to Mrs. Lee, Mei Ling's mother, who lived next door to us.

"I hope so," Mei Ling's mother sighed. "I need a good brew. The rent is due. Woody told me he will be back this evening. But you know Woody. The two girls will have to stand watch if Woody misses the bus or something."

Police Raid on Moonshine Pond

I snuggled closer to Mei Ling. At eleven, Mei Ling was a year older than me.

A man walked up the dark street from the direction of Calcutta. His steps crunched the gravel and kicked up fine dust from the road. He wore a shawl over his head. As he passed the street light, we saw that the man was not Woody. A dog from the garbage heap followed the man for half a block and returned to the garbage.

A dog from the Chung tannery barked. All the tanneries and houses kept "guard" dogs, friendly dogs that barked at both friends and strangers.

The dogs at the garbage heap answered the Chung dog. Other dogs joined in. A door across the street opened and Mrs. Liu looked at us. We shook our heads and smiled. She waved and shut the door. Babies cried and voices hushed the dogs.

The barking stopped. One lone dog howled.

"I read in a book that in America and Europe, Santa Claus runs around on the rooftops on Christmas day," I said. "He rides around in a dog sled and he slides down holes in the roofs. He is a noisy person. He keeps saying, 'Ho, ho, ho.'"

Mei Ling laughed. "You think he will slide down the smoke hole in the shack shouting, 'Ho, ho, ho?'"

"Our mothers will put him to work. That will quieten him." We laughed and huddled closer.

"Mother told me there is no Santa Claus," said Mei Ling.

"In the picture book, Santa looks a lot like the God of Long Life, or the laughing Buddha. They all laugh a lot," I said.

Mei Ling thought for a moment and shook her head. "Nah. Santa has a lot of hair and a thick, long, curly beard. The God of Long Life has a shiny, domed head and white eyebrows that curve around the sides of his eyes and end at his shoulders."

"Maybe Santa is the younger brother of the God of Long Life," I said. "He spends a lot of time giving presents to strangers."

We meditated on the strange behaviour of this strange God.

I gripped Mei Ling's hand as we heard the wheezing murmur of a car engine. Few people travel in Tangra at night by car. A set of headlights swung around the curve of the road.

We relaxed. Police cars usually turned their headlights off for night raids. The car swept past and showered us with dust and grit.

I pressed my knees tighter to my chest and held a corner of my skirt over my nose. From the Lin Tannery, a clock struck eleven times.

A gust showered us with more dust and grit and almost blew our skirts over our heads.

I pushed my skirt down. "I wish we had Santa Claus' coat. We would both be warm."

Another car roared around the curve of the road, its headlight's off.

Mei Ling and I slid off the bench and scurried behind a pile of lumber. We slipped through a small doorway into Mr. Chung's tannery.

We shut and bolted the door and waited. The Chung dog came over and sniffed our shoes. We heard the car stop at the main gate of the Chung tannery. Heavy boots crunched on the gravel.

"Police! Open the door." The heavy wooden door shuddered from the kicks and bangs.

Mei Ling and I looked at each other, turned and ran. The dog ran with us and barked and growled. Dogs in the neighbouring tanneries barked and howled.

The tannery, without the daytime hum and clatter of machinery and men's chatter, now lay dark and silent. Mei Ling and I ran past hidestretching machines, jumped over piles of leather, tripped over cables, knocked over pails and left a trail of nails, water and overturned chemical cans.

We reached the back door of the tannery. The dog stopped inside the doorway and barked. We stumbled outside. The cold wind swept around the building and pushed us against the tannery wall.

"I can't see the pathway between the ponds." Mei Ling's voice wavered. We had left our flashlight beside the bench, outside the tannery.

"I think the pond covered over with the Chung tannery's drying boards is on our left," I said.

"Yes. The open pond is on our right." Mei Ling grabbed my hand. "I can't swim," she wailed.

We held hands and ran. We tripped and we fell and got up again. The dogs barked, whined and howled.

"Open the door or we will break it down!" The bangs on the door got louder.

"Shut up. We are trying to sleep here," someone shouted from the living quarters upstairs in the Chung tannery.

We hurried on. I tripped on a pothole and fell. Tears ran down my face. My knees ached, my left palm stung and my sides hurt. Mei Ling pulled me up and gasped, "Hurry!"

We held hands and we ran. Mei Ling tripped. I screamed and went down with her. "We have to hurry," Mei Ling sobbed. We got up and hurried on.

As we neared the shack, we shouted, "Police! Police!" We stopped, sobbed and gasped for breath inside the shack. The warmth and the smoke enveloped us.

The workers in the shack had heard the shouts and the dogs before we got there. Everyone rushed to hide the moonshine. Mother pulled the tube from a half-filled bottle, slammed a cork into its mouth, hugged it to her chest and ran through the courtyard. My elder brother, Nan, picked up two corked bottles, snatched a flashlight from a bench and followed Mother. I ran after them. Other shadowy figures ran in the same direction. Lights from their flashlights bounced above the footpath like fireflies.

Inside the shack, the fires burned low and fermented brew bubbled. The rubber tubes that fed into bottles lay on the floor. Alcohol ran in little streams onto the dirt floor and flowed towards the pond. The moonshiners hid the Chinese moonshine in the ponds around the building. Dots of light from the flashlights danced on the edges of the ponds.

Mother walked slowly back to the courtyard. I followed. The policemen's flashlights played across the pathway between the two ponds and their footsteps crunched on the loose gravel. Mother looked me over. She wiped my face with her apron, brushed the dirt and grit from my clothes and pushed me towards our apartment. "You two did very well tonight. Change your clothes and then go to bed. I will clean you up properly later."

I saw Mei Ling walk towards her apartment, next door to ours. We smiled at each other and she said, "Now we can be warm."

The sticky, sweet smell of fermentation filled the apartment. Barley and raw sugar for next week's batch of moonshine fermented under the bed. I pulled a blanket over myself and sneezed when a stiff woollen thread tickled my nose. I heard shouting from the shack. "Whose bottles are these? Come on, they belong to one of you."

Police Raid on Moonshine Pond

Mr. Tan, another moonshiner, asked, "What bottles? What are you talking about?"

"Okay. So you want to play games. I know you have brewed a lot of alcohol tonight. We will look for it."

I heard doors bang and more shouting. A policeman marched into our apartment. Mother followed him.

"Please don't wake my daughter," Mother said. "She is not well."

"I want to see your papers," the policeman said.

Mother went to the cupboard and took out a bundle wrapped in oilskin. She opened it and took out her visa that allowed her to stay in Calcutta. I saw Mother fold some money into the visa as she handed it to the policeman.

The policeman walked to the light. He held the papers upside down. His hands slid from the papers to his pocket. He handed the visa back to mother. "Papers seem okay."

He opened a few cupboard doors, glanced under the bed and puckered his lips. Mother handed him more money. The policeman left the apartment. I heard him say to someone, "That apartment is clean. Nothing there."

Outside, geese squawked as policemen rummaged through their nest in the courtyard. A policeman shouted. He had found the two bottles of alcohol Mrs. Lee had left for them.

Woody and Mei Ling

Two weeks after the police raid, I stood at the gates of the courtyard overlooking the fish farm. Palm trees fringed the checkerboard of ponds. The morning mist curled on the surface of the water.

A man walked on the footpath between the ponds. Over his shoulder, he carried a long pole with a net at the end. He stopped, peered into a pond and poised the net above the surface. The net blurred as the man dipped the net quickly into the water and came up with a fish. The fish wriggled in the net as the man rested the pole over his shoulder. He walked along the footpath and disappeared under the palm trees.

I took a deep breath. The mist swallowed the dust and softened the sounds around me. A cock crowed. Sparrows quarrelled over worms under some bushes. A dog barked. Mrs. Chiu's geese splashed into the pond on my right. Dew sparkled and winked on the grass. I shifted my school bag on my shoulder.

A breeze cleared the mist in front of me. A sliver of mist floated past. I reached out and felt the cool mist melt on my palm. I closed my fingers.

"Hey, are you coming or not?" Woody shouted from the gate leading to the main road. Mei Ling, his sister, stood beside him.

"Coming." I turned and ran towards Woody and Mei Ling.

I attended a school in Calcutta's Chinatown, about ten miles from Tangra. On school days, I stayed with my brother Panda who lived and worked in our shoe shop in Calcutta. Every Saturday afternoon, I took the bus to Tangra with Mother. Mother lived and brewed moonshine in Tangra. She usually took me to school on Monday mornings. That week, both she and Mrs. Lee, Mei Ling's mother, caught the flu. Mother asked Woody to take me to school in Calcutta.

I stopped, stared at Woody and giggled. Mei Ling giggled too. Woody scowled. He wore a loose short-sleeved shirt, buttoned at the front. The buttons pulled tight over his stomach. Woody looked like a pregnant scarecrow.

I lifted a corner of his shirt and saw black rubber tubing. Woody had wound a length of rubber tubing filled with Chinese moonshine around his middle. Only one bus line travelled between Calcutta and Tangra and the police would wait at the bus stop. When women smuggled moonshine to customers in Calcutta, they wound moonshine-filled tubing around their stomachs and pretended to be pregnant. Woody tried to look fat, but he looked more like a stick figure with a bloated middle.

"Come on. It is hard work being fat." Woody reached down for the openweave, plastic shopping basket at his feet.

Woody hugged a basketball wrapped in a towel. He put the basketball into the basket. The basketball was filled with moonshine. The handle of the basket stretched when Woody picked it up. Woody waddled down the footpath. Mei Ling and I followed. We nudged each other and giggled. Woody muttered, "I wish mother was not sick. She is much better at this than I am. At least the police would not dare search her."

A policeman once tried to search a woman. The crowd stopped him, beat him up and chased him for three blocks. Both Hindus and Muslims had a moral and religious taboo against a man touching a woman who was not his wife.

We met Woody's friend Sean. "Congratulations!" Sean laughed. "When is the baby due?"

Woody swung the basket at Sean. "Shut up. I am fat, that's all. Fat."

Sean looked Woody over. "You don't look fat, you know. You look like you are carrying a fat snake under your shirt."

Mei Ling and I laughed.

Sean walked with us. His mother had sent him to the market in Tapsia, a half-hour walk from the Moonshine Pond.

"I missed the cock fight last week. How did it go?" Sean asked.

Woody kept two fighting cocks. Cock fights were illegal. When the police raided the fights, they confiscated the betting money and the birds.

Woody shrugged. "It went okay. My bird won."

"Are you sure? You sounded like you lost. What happened?"

Woody switched the basket to the other hand. "You know that we held the cock fight in the crematorium, the one by the Hoogly River?"

Sean nodded.

"That crematorium was just a flat piece of land with nothing on it. Except for ashes. As we drew a circle for the birds to fight in, two funeral groups arrived. They set up their wood pyres and started to burn the bodies. The relatives stood around; they cried and wailed. Well, we got as far as we could from the burnings. The wind blew the smoke in our direction. I did not notice the smell at the time. I was too busy with the cocks. We cheered and shouted as the cocks fought. One of the Indians came over and told us to be quiet. We did not listen, of course." Woody stopped and swallowed. His Adam's apple bobbed.

"Well? So what happened?" Sean asked.

Woody looked sick. "Nothing happened. There was a lot of smoke from the pyres. The smell of the burning bodies stayed with me. I could not eat for three days. I threw up every time I smelled cooked meat. It was awful."

Sean snickered. "Serves you right. Why didn't you people fight in St. Paul's Cemetery? It's a nice, quiet spot."

"The police came and raided us when we held a fight in St. Paul's a month ago. You know how Chou liked to perch on the tombstone to watch the fight? Well, when the police burst in through the gates, Chou fell off the tomb-stone and broke his wrist. Ki tripped on another tombstone and bloodied his nose. Those tombstones are dangerous. Anyway, we decided to try the crematorium." Woody shuddered. "But never again."

"Lovely. So you had morning sickness and now you are pregnant." Chuckling, Sean turned onto a side road towards the market.

Woody yelled at Sean's back. "I told you I am fat, not pregnant." Mei Ling and I laughed as we walked down Tangra Road.

We reached the bus stop. Stalls fanned out from a large banyan tree. Ram had his tea stall on one side of the banyan tree. He sat cross-legged on a low bench. Clay cups stacked under his seat. A large kettle boiled on a coal-burning stove. A wok of milk simmered on a smaller stove. A glass display case protected raisin buns, puff pastries and Indian sweets from the dust and flies. A picture of the Hindu god Shiva, framed by garlands of plastic flowers, hung on the tree beside Ram. Two rickety wooden benches faced the tea stall.

Piles of broken clay cups surrounded the benches. Ram served tea in unglazed clay cups. The customers threw the cups away when they finished their tea.

On the other side of the tree, Chandra sold deep-fried vegetables. He coated slices of potato, onion and cauliflower with chickpea flour paste and fried them in a deep cast-iron wok. The wok sat on a coal-fire stove. Chandra sat cross-legged on a bench. His left hand dipped the slices of vegetable in the batter and dropped pieces into the bubbling hot oil in the wok. His right hand grasped the greasy wooden handle of a metal scoop, lifted the cooked pieces out of the wok and onto a metal tray lined with newspaper. Mei Ling and I loved Chandra's battered vegetables.

The vegetable- and fruit-stall vendors fanned their goods with folded newspapers and fans made of palm leaves to chase away the flies. The peanut vendor added pieces of coal to his stove. He stirred the sand and unshelled peanuts in his wok.

Over thirty people waited for the bus. The passengers stood around and talked. Some of them chewed betel and spat. The ground around the bus stop was red with pan spittings. In a stall, a *pan-walla* chopped betel, vanilla, cinnamon sticks and other spices, trimmed fresh leaves and wrapped the nuts and spices in the leaves. One pan-chewing woman smiled at me, her teeth stained red with betel juice.

Women yelled and chased after children who ran and screamed at each other and tripped over parcels and bags. At the back of the bus stop, a woman bathed under the spout of the hand pump. Her seven-year-old daughter held the heavy handle. She jumped up and pushed down on the handle. Water gushed as she pumped. Her mother soaped herself and the sari she wore, then rinsed off under the water.

A policeman in a once-white uniform sat on the bench at the tea stall. He sipped from a clay cup. His cudgel leaned against his left leg.

"Come, I will get you some snacks." Woody grabbed Mei Ling's hand and pulled her towards Chandra's stall, away from the policeman. I followed.

Mei Ling and I stood near Chandra's stall. We each ate pieces of fried potatoes, carrots and cauliflowers from a small, oil-stained bag made of newspaper. Woody glanced at the policeman from the corner of his eyes. He muttered, "Bus, please come, please, please, please."

The policeman walked towards Chandra's stall. Woody grabbed Mei Ling's hand and walked around the tree towards Ram's tea stall. I dropped the bag of fried vegetables, ran and tried to keep up. The policeman called out, "You, *Cheena* boy, stop. I want to talk to you." Woody walked faster. Mei Ling ran to keep up. The policeman ran past me. Woody turned to face the policeman. I held on to my school bag and stopped behind a woman who sat on a bench, surrounded by her shopping bags.

The policeman came up to Woody. "What is in that basket?"

"My basketball." Woody hugged the basket.

"Hand it over. I want to see it." The policeman shifted his cudgel in his hand and eyed Woody's budging middle.

"Why? It is my basketball. I need it for the game today." Woody stepped away.

"Come on. I want the basket. Hand it over." The policeman moved toward him and waved his cudgel.

Woody reached into the basket and pulled out a knife. The policeman stepped back. He raised his cudgel.

Woody and Mei Ling

Woody plunged the knife into the basketball. Liquid squirted. The Chinese moonshine hit Mei Ling on the face and ran down the front of her school uniform. She gasped, hugged her middle and sat down on the dusty ground, amidst the broken clay cups, stained food wrappings and spilled tea.

Woody threw the still-squirting basketball at the policeman. The policeman, his eyes wide, caught the ball. Woody shouted, "What have you done to my sister?"

The policeman held the deflated basketball against his chest. Brown liquid splattered his chest and trickled down to his pants.

Mei Ling coughed and retched. Moonshine ran down her hair, her arms and her uniform. She rubbed her eyes with her handkerchief and sobbed. I walked over, picked up her school bag and squatted beside her. A crowd gathered. A woman asked Mei Ling, "What happened? Are you sick?"

Mei Ling looked at me and hiccupped. She heaved and her breakfast pooled around her.

Woody stood beside Mei Ling. He shouted at the policeman. "What have you done to my sister? What did you throw at her?"

Mei Ling moaned. "I feel dizzy. I feel very sick." She hiccupped again and retched. I patted her shoulder. My hand came away sticky. I took out my handkerchief and wiped Mei Ling's face.

Woody, his arms on his hips, stalked up to the policeman and waved his fist. "I want to talk to your supervisor. I want to tell him about you. I want to tell him how you bullied my sister. How could you? She is only ten-years-old."

A man by the tea stall said, "Shame on you. Go bother someone else." Another man shook his fist at the policeman.

The policeman threw down the limp basketball and backed toward the road. A woman picked up a broken clay cup and threw it at him. A banana peel hit the policeman on the temple. Two ripe tomatoes splattered his stomach and a stone bounced off his chest. The policeman turned and ran. The crowd booed and jeered.

The bus, packed with passengers, turned the corner. People hung out of the front and back doorways of the bus. Five men stood on the back bumper, their arms locked around the back window frames. Two boys lay on their stomachs on the roof, their arms wrapped around parcels. The bus shuddered and stopped in front of the tea stall. Black smoke and dust hovered. The passengers going to Calcutta crowded around the doorway, while the passengers coming from Calcutta pushed and shoved to get off. The bus driver, his assistant and two conductors strolled toward the tea stall, bought tea and sat down on the bench.

Woody carried Mei Ling to the hand pump. The woman moved aside. Woody smiled at the girl at the handle of the pump and wet his handkerchief. He washed Mei Ling's face, rinsed out the cloth and wiped Mei Ling's uniform.

"Are you feeling better now?" Woody peered at Mei Ling's face. "Next time, don't hold on to my hand. I may have to run from the policeman. I was going to throw the ball at him and run. You won't be able to keep up with me. So next time, you stay by the bus stop until I get back. Okay? I am sorry I splashed you. You will feel better in a little while."

Mei Ling hiccupped. Woody dusted Mei Ling's skirt and wiped her shoes. The bus driver finished his tea and walked towards the bus.

Woody patted Mei Ling's head. "Okay now? Let's get on the bus. The policeman may be back."

The bus driver sounded the horn. We ran. I climbed onto the bus. Woody lifted Mei Ling and followed. I squeezed past two men and their bags by the door and climbed over two cloth-wrapped bundles in the aisle as I headed toward the ladies-only seats. All buses and trams in Calcutta had seats reserved for women. During the morning and evening rush hours, the tram routes from the government offices had trams for women passengers only. My sister, Lady, and I always tried to get on ladies-only trams.

I looked at the two men who sat on the ladies-only seats and told them that my friend and I wanted to sit down. They stared out the window and pretended not to hear. I said again, "You are sitting in the ladies-only seats."

The two men looked at Mei Ling and me, sighed, gathered their bags and stood up. Woody lifted Mei Ling onto the seat by the window and said, "If you feel sick again, put your head out the window."

I scrambled up beside her.

Mei Ling leaned her head against the window and closed her eyes. I touched her hand and asked, "Are you feeling better? Do you want something to eat?"

Mei Ling shook her head. "I feel a little dizzy. I want to sleep." Mei Ling slept with her head on my shoulder. Her head rolled forward and back when the bus hit pot-holes. I wedged Mei Ling against the side of the bus and held her there with my shoulder.

Woody left Mei Ling in my brother's shoe shop and delivered the Chinese moonshine. Mei Ling slept on my bed when I left for school.

That evening, I sat on my concrete seat on the rooftop terrace of my brother's shoe shop, with my school books piled beside me. My brother Panda kept his pigeons and cock-birds on the terrace. In the coops, pigeons cooed over their evening feed. Sitting on the floor with a cock-bird on his lap, my brother cooed at the bird.

The clanging of the trams on the street mingled with bus and car horns. The curses of the drivers mixed with the voices of the vendors shouting their wares. The vendor who sold sugarcane juice had a loud voice. "Sahib, come and quench your thirst. Very good juice."

I smelled the roasted peanuts and my stomach rumbled.

Woody climbed up the ladder. Panda waved him over. "What did you do to my sister this morning?" my brother asked.

Woody sniggered. "Nothing. You should have seen what I did to *my* sister this morning."

Panda slapped Woody on the shoulder. "You should be ashamed of yourself. Getting your sister drunk. What did your mother say to that?"

"My mother felt relieved that I delivered half the brew. We needed money for rent." Woody chuckled. "My sister was sicker than a dog. She will not be drinking for a long time."

Panda pounded Woody on the back and they chortled.

I shouted, "It is not funny. Mei Ling was very sick. She had to miss school today and it is all your fault."

Panda turned to me and said, "Sorry, little one. I forgot you were there."

Woody nudged Panda, "You should have seen the policeman. He could have outrun a cheetah." They laughed again.

Panda stroked his cock-bird. "Woody, how did your cock do in the fight last week?"

Woody groaned.

I bent over my exercise book as my brother and Woody talked about the cock fights. The sky darkened. Woody and Panda talked and laughed in the dark.

After two years of pretending to be pregnant and dealing with police raids, Mother gave up brewing moonshine. She went back to Calcutta, and once again, sold bean sprouts and salted vegetables.

The Godfather of Chinatown

Chattawalla Gully, a narrow lane, runs from Sun Yat Sen Street to Bow Bazaar Street. *Chatta* means umbrella in Hindi. In the 1800s, Muslims, Jews and Parsees lived in Chattawalla Gully. They made and sold umbrellas. The Chinese moved into Chattawalla Gully in the early twentieth century.

My family lived at 14/1 Chattawalla Gully. From above, the building looked like a square doughnut with a central courtyard in the doughnut hole. The apartments' entrances opened into the courtyard. The only window of our apartment faced the back doors of a row of one-storied shops. The shopfronts opened onto Sun Yat Sen Street. When the Calcutta Municipal Corporation demolished the shops, the window of my family's apartment overlooked Sun Yat Sen Street and a large vacant lot across the street. The lot, the size of a football field, stayed empty for more than ten years.

The poor untouchables, Hindus of the lowest caste, moved onto the vacant lot. They recovered cardboard, plywood, plastic sheets and newspapers from the garbage dumps and lashed the pieces together with frayed pieces of rope onto bamboo or wooden frames to build shacks. The untouchables cooked over wood fires on the sidewalk or sometimes on the street and used the gutters as lavatories and bathing areas.

From the rooftop terrace on the third floor of my apartment building, the vacant lot looked like a dirty tattered patchwork of greys and dull browns. Faded laundry and cow-dung patties crowded the roofs of the shacks. The untouchables used the dried patties as fuel and sold the excess. Narrow footpaths zigzagged between rows of sagging shacks. Naked children played in small pools of slimy water on the footpaths. Women squatted before wood and cowdung cooking fires.

Across from our window, prostitutes built small lean-tos to serve their customers. These women wore bright saris, rouged their cheeks and lips and lined their eyes with kohl. When they had no customers, they sat outside their lean-tos and combed each other's hair with finetoothed combs that removed lice.

Coolies, lavatory cleaners and labourers who earned a few cents during the day, visited prostitutes at night. These men drank cheap, illegally brewed alcohol and curled up in a doorway or on the pavement until dawn.

The children of the prostitutes lived on the streets. They roamed the marketplace, picked pockets and stole from customers and shopkeepers. Most grew up to be prostitutes and coolies.

Anarkali

At midnight, I finished my assignment on the Japanese Invasion of Nanking for Mr. Thai, our history teacher. I blew out the candle and rubbed my eyes. The Calcutta Electric Supply Corporation (CESC) had cut the power earlier in the evening. Usually I studied at my school friend Kwan's apartment. The supply line to her apartment also supplied electricity to the Eden Hospital. The CESC did not cut power to police stations and hospitals.

The Godfather of Chinatown

My one-year-old nephew whimpered in the next room. My sister-in-law spoke softly to him and he quietened. I picked up the flashlight and walked into the kitchen for a drink of water. I stood by the wiremesh door and looked out into the courtyard. Itchy, Mr. Lai's dog, sprawled by Mr. Lai's door. He opened his eyes and cocked his left ear at me and then went back to sleep. A cockroach scurried across the floor by my feet. I stomped and missed. The full moon rose over the edge of the terrace and peeped into the courtyard. The moon threw its soft light on the peeling stucco and the cracked drainpipes along the side of the building. The communal garbage pile hid in the shadow. A rat ran across the courtyard and passed near Itchy's nose. Itchy snored.

"Lazy dog," I muttered.

Whack! Mr. Lai, two doors down, hit one of his prostitutes. "Stupid cow! You think you can cheat me?"

Whack! "I told you I wanted all the money. You think you can lie to me?" Whack! A woman screamed. Mr. Lai yelled, "I will kill you!"

"I am sorry, sahib," the woman whimpered. "I am sorry. I won't do it again." I recognized Anarkali's voice. Five years ago, she moved into the lean-to across the road. She called herself Anarkali, the name of a popular Bollywood movie about a courtesan called Anarkali who died for love.

"You won't do it again is right. I won't give you the chance. Get out! Get out! Get out of here." A thud sounded from the street.

Mr. Lai, a bald, fat man in his forties, moved into the Bow Bazaar area in the 1940s. He ran a gambling house on Guru Nanak Street, in the New Market district. He was also the *dada*, the pimp, for the prostitutes on Sun Yat Sen Street. Mr. Lai told the prostitutes that he protected them. He bribed the police for them, he looked after the violent customers and he kept the other pimps from the area. Every night, Mr. Lai watched by his window. When a prostitute finished with a customer, she handed Mr. Lai half her money through a slot in the window. Mr. Lai also took in betting money from his window seat.

My nephews cried in the next room. My mother woke and sat up. Itchy barked and ran in circles in the courtyard.

I hurried over to the window and looked out. Mr. Lai shook his fist at Anarkali. Anarkali, an older prostitute, attracted little business and knew that Mr. Lai would get rid of her soon. The older prostitutes always tried to keep back some money from Mr. Lai.

Anarkali lay on the cracked and dirty pavement, her hands wrapped around her head. She cringed when Mr. Lai moved towards her. Sweat ran down Mr. Lai's head. His shirt front stuck on the sweat of his overhanging belly.

Mr. Lai's Chinese wife called out to him. "Let the woman go. I am sure she's learned her lesson."

Mr. Lai spat on Anarkali and stalked back to his apartment. I heard his wife offer him a cup of tea.

Mr. Lai had two wives and eleven children. He started as a messenger boy in a gambling house when he was ten-years-old. He became a pimp at sixteen. At eighteen, he eloped with a seventeen-year-old girl. Mr. and Mrs. Liang, the girl's parents, disowned her. Six years later, he met a Nepalese girl and set her up in a third floor apartment. His Chinese wife, who lived on the ground floor in the same building, protested. Mr. Lai beat his Chinese wife and told her to go back to her parents. The Chinese Mrs. Lai stayed. The two wives avoided each other.

The Godfather of Chinatown

Anarkali had a clear voice and she loved to sing. I used to fall asleep with Anarkali crooning, "*Ye zindagi*....," the song from the movie *Anarkali*, the song that the courtesan sang as the maharajah's men entombed her alive.

That night, Anarkali did not sing. She sobbed quietly.

The next morning, in front of her lean-to, with her right eye swollen shut, her head bowed and her shoulders slumped, Anarkali sat motionless as the shantytown dwellers woke to a grey dawn. Another prostitute sat beside her. Both in their mid-twenties, the prostitutes looked thirty years older.

A week later, Anarkali disappeared. A twelve-year-old girl, Jasmine, took over Anarkali's lean-to. Jasmin wore red saris and had jasmine flowers braided into her hair. Mr. Lai was pleased. Many customers visited Jasmine. Six months later, Mr. Lai shouted and beat Jasmine. She was pregnant. Twelve months after she moved into the shantytown on Sun Yat Sen Street, Jasmine gave birth to a daughter in her lean-to.

I saw Anarkali once more, six months after she disappeared from Sun Yat Sen Street. Anarkali sat outside the Kali temple, among the beggars. She slouched, grey and still, like the wall behind her. Her sunken eyes stared at the tin can in front of her on the cracked and dirty pavement.

I looked into the temple. The painted straw-and-clay image of Kali, Goddess of Destruction, Death and Sorrow, glared at me. Crimson blood streaked Kali's black and gleaming body. A garland of clay human heads bracketed her bare breasts. Kali's left foot pressed down on a clay male figure lying in a pool of vivid red paint. More red paint covered the figure's pale body.

I smelt the blood of the black goat left on the altar, its throat slit. Someone had made a blood sacrifice to the goddess. Two priests beat drums and chanted. A child, her thumb in her mouth, tried to hide behind her mother. The mother prostrated before Kali and offered flowers and money to the goddess. One of the priests smiled, showing stained and chipped teeth. "Kali bless you."

The mother bowed low toward the priest and dragged her daughter forward for his blessing. The child struggled, pulled on her mother's sari and cried. On either side of the image, worshippers lined the walls. They clapped their hands and swayed in time with their chants. The priest threw a handful of incense into the fire. I sneezed and my eyes watered as the smoke rose.

A passerby spat at Anakali's can and missed. "Stupid beggar." He kicked the can.

I put coins in Anakali's can and moved it against her knee. She stared at the ground.

As I waited for the traffic lights to change, I looked back. Thick incense smoke drifted from the temple. I could no longer see Anarkali.

The Cockerel

The Chinese families living at 14/1 Chattawalla Gully kept hens in the courtyard, mainly for eggs. Before going to school, I fed the six hens we owned. Every morning, the hens stood by the screen door, pecked at the hens nearest them and looked for me. They muttered as they waited.

Mother set aside the previous night's leftover dinner for the hens. I filled one bowl with the leftover rice and vegetables and filled another bowl with wheat. I placed the bowls on the floor and opened the screen door to let the hens into the kitchen. All the hens in the courtyard rushed in. I yelled and tried to chase the neighbours' hens from the kitchen, scaring most of the hens away, including the ones I wanted to feed.

My favourite hen, Chips, was the lowest on the pecking order. The other hens always chased her away from the feeding bowls. I often held Chips on my lap with the feeding bowl so that she ate.

Mr. Lai had a cockerel. The cockerel crowed constantly and chased the hens. It liked to stand on our chicken coop and preen itself. Once a week I had to clean the cockerel's droppings off the top of the chicken coop. As Mr. Lai's cockerel grew old, the other hens could run from him. So the cockerel picked on Chips.

When the cockerel was six years old and blind in one eye, Mrs. Wong, our neighbour, bought another cockerel. The Wong cockerel's feathers shone like the brass fittings of the Grand Hotel on Chowringhee, its beak and claws pointed and sharp like the knife that Mr. Lai carried and its crown and wattles rosy like Jasmin's cheeks and lips.

The Wong cockerel eyed the hens. He extended his neck, opened his beak and crowed a challenge. When the Lai cockerel did not respond, the Wong cockerel minced towards the Lai cockerel. The Lai cockerel fluffed its tattered neck feathers, stretched its wings and charged the Wong cockerel.

People jammed the windows and apartment doorways around the courtyard. We clapped, cheered and jeered as wings flapped, feet raked, beaks slashed and feathers flew.

The Wong cockerel jumped onto the back of the Lai cockerel. Its claws dug into the sparse feathers and bony back of the Lai cockerel. The Wong cockerel opened its beak and clamped down hard on the Lai cockerel's wattles. The Lai cockerel bucked, but the Wong cockerel hung on. Blood flew. The Lai cockerel screeched with pain. He banged into the garbage can. The Wong cockerel let go and flew on top of the garbage can. The Lai cockerel fled under its coop. The Wong cockerel, its head held high, strutted and crowed.

The people around the courtyard cheered.

Mr. Lai grabbed his cockerel from under the chicken coop and threw it at the Wong cockerel. The Wong cockerel pecked hard at the Lai cockerel's wattles and chased it around the courtyard until the Lai cockerel hid again beneath the chicken coop.

Hands on his hips, Mr. Lai stomped to the middle of the courtyard. He called out to Mr. Wong. "Lou Wong, you'd better get rid of your cockerel, it is creating a disturbance."

Mr. Wong came to his door. "Well, the birds are settling in. They will be good friends in no time."

Mr. Lai shook his head. "No. Get rid of your bird. My cockerel was here first."

Mr. Wong looked doubtful. "Well, you know, your bird was getting a little slow. Maybe it is time for a younger bird."

Mr. Lai's eyes narrowed. "My bird is not getting old. You get rid of your bird. Or I will."

Mr. Wong scratched his head and looked down at his feet. "But, I don't want to...."

Mrs. Wong came out of the apartment. She touched Mr. Wong on the arm. "It's okay, Mr. Lai. I planned to have chicken stew this week. The cockerel will do nicely. I will look after this matter."

Mr. Lai grunted and walked towards his apartment. At the door, he turned and said, "Get rid of it today."

The Wong cockerel went into the stew pot that evening.

The Godfather of Chinatown

The Police and Mr. Lai

Everyone in Chattawalla Gully feared Mr. Lai. He collected protection money from vendors and shopkeepers on our street, he collected rent money from the shantytown dwellers, he sided with gangs who paid him and beat up those who refused. He also took over the rooftop terrace. My mother and the other Chinese in the building gave him presents so that we could use the terrace. We strung wire across the terrace to dry our clothes. At New Year's and festivals, Mother and the other neighbours visited Mr. Lai with packages of fruits and cakes. When I was twelve years old, I stood outside Mr. Lai's doorway and watched the ritual.

Mr. Lai sat on a high armchair, his feet on a wooden footrest. He laughed and flashed his gold-plated incisors. The corners of his mouth slanted high into his cheekbones and his eyes crinkled into narrow slits. The Chinese Mrs. Lai sat on a stool beside him. His children ran in and out of the apartment. They chased and tripped over each other, shouted, laughed and screamed. The neighbours sat on stools facing Mr. Lai.

"The neighbourhood used to be bad before you came," Mrs. Lim, who lived next door to us, said.

Mr. Wong nodded. "There used to be many thieves around here. I remember once someone stole all my towels drying on the terrace, after my wife spent hours washing them."

Mr. Lai laughed. His eyes crinkled shut. His mouth opened wide and his tonsils wobbled. "If any thieves dare to come back to our area, I will kill them. You let me know if anything gets stolen from our area. I will find the thief."

"Oh, good," I said from the doorway, "Someone took our best egg-laying hen last week. Could you find the hen for us?"

Mr. Lai lost his smile.

Mother gave me a stern look. "I think the hen wandered off. I am sure it will find its way back one of these days." She turned back to Mr. Lai. "Yes, Mr. Lai, how is business in your betting place?" Mr. Lai ran a gambling den in New Market, three miles from Chattawalla Gully.

Mr. Lai's face creased into a wide smile. "Business is very good. Thank the Buddha. The police came a few times, but I chased them away."

"Do the police come often?" asked Mrs. Wong.

Mr. Lai waved his hand. The three rings on his fingers flashed. "Nah. They are afraid of me, you see. I am very friendly with the police superintendent. Now and then I let the police raid my place. They take a few rupees for tea money. Keeps them happy." He laughed. His visitors laughed.

Three months ago, the police had arrested Mr. Lai. His two wives had cried and moaned and visited him every day. His Chinese wife had gone to the neighbours and borrowed enough money to get him out. When Mr. Lai had returned home, he stayed in bed, moaned and whimpered. His two wives ran to his every sound. They cooled his brow, rubbed soothing ointment on his bruises, cooked his favourite food and held his hands while he slept. The Lai kitchen steamed with ginseng tea and Chinese herbal brew. The Nepalese Mrs. Lai told Mother that the police beat him every day he was jailed. He could not walk. His feet and ankles were swollen. The police beat the soles of his feet with metal rods. He had bruises all over his body. He stayed in bed for three weeks.

"This year I donated five hundred rupees to the temple and spent another five hundred on the wall hangings behind the altar," said Mr. Lai. "The gods will look after me this year, I am sure. I am also donating to the Chinese Widow and Orphan Fund and The Temple

Renovation Fund. Someone has to look after our people." Mr. Lai folded his hands on his lap. "Mr. Lo from the Chinese Club said that I am the most generous member of the club. He even showed me the donation book. No one gave more than I." Mr. Lai beamed.

I later asked Mother if we get money from the Chinese Widow and Orphan Fund. Mother looked shocked. "Of course not. We are not destitute. We do not need charity. In fact, I donate to the fund."

Mr. Banerjee

Every winter, Tibetan traders came through the pass near Darjeeling to Calcutta. They brought carved stone trinkets, blankets, shawls and sweaters to sell at the open air market in the Maidan. Mr. Lai rented out the rooftop terrace as a camp site for the Tibetans. For a month, thirty or forty Tibetans lived on the terrace. They cooked on smoky woodfires and slept in nests of colorful blankets. Prayer flags flew from bamboo poles. The sour smell of unwashed bodies, the rattle of the prayer wheels and the chanting of mantras drifted down to the courtyard every morning.

Mr. Banerjee, our landlord, once tried to collect some of the terrace rent money from Mr. Lai. Twenty-five years old, Mr. Banerjee attended Calcutta University. He wore fine cotton Nehru shirts and dhotis, a loincloth. In winter, he draped a cashmere shawl around his shoulders. His dreamy eyes and soft voice were more suited to Rabindranath Tagore poetry recitals than rent collection.

The tenants had their rent money ready for Mr. Banerjee on the first day of each month. Mr. Banerjee spent five minutes with each tenant. Every month, when Mr. Bannerjee walked into our apartment, Mother handed over the money. Mr. Banerjee would count the bills, then hand Mother a receipt.

On a cool January morning, Jade, my neighbour and school friend, and I sat on low stools in the courtyard, two yards from the Lai apartment door. We chatted as we shelled peas. Mr. Banerjee walked into Mr. Lai's apartment and closed the door.

Jade and I looked at each other. Mr. Banerjee never closed doors on his rent collection runs. We moved our stools closer to the Lai apartment door.

We heard Mr. Lai's voice. "Why should I give you the terrace money? I work hard to get the Tibetans comfortable and they come back every year. I look after them day and night; I pay to have the terrace cleaned. I pay to have water up there. What did you do?"

We heard Mr. Banerjee murmur.

Mr. Lai raised his voice. "So? I don't care if you own the building. I don't care if you own the whole city. You fat cats are all the same. You sit on your arse and do nothing. Then you try to take the hard-earned money from the poor."

Mr. Banerjee murmured again.

Mr. Lai shouted. "No. No. No. You are lucky I don't charge you for looking after your building so well. I am not giving you any of the terrace money. Not a single rupee. Not a single pisa. What are you going to do about it?"

Mr. Banerjee murmured yet again.

Something crashed. Something heavy hit the floor. Mr. Lai screamed. "You will call the police? You will call police? You dirty dog! You filthy son-of-a-bitch! *I will give you some real reason to call the police!*"

Jade and I picked up our stools and the bowls of peas and moved against the wall.

The door crashed open and Mr. Banerjee dashed out. The end of his cashmere shawl dragged across the ground. Mr. Lai, waving a meat cleaver, thundered after Mr. Banerjee, his face purple with rage. His eyes bulged and foam and spittle ran down the corners of his mouth. Mr. Banerjee ran out of the building.

Itchy barked and bounded towards the noise. He ran after Mr. Banerjee, stopped at the front door of the building and barked. Mr. Lai ran into Itchy, tripped over Itchy's paws and fell. The cleaver nipped Itchy's tail. Itchy yelped, ran under a chicken coop and whimpered.

Mr. Lai's wives and children avoided him that day. We did not see him for the rest of the week. The Chinese Mrs. Lai told Mother that Mr. Lai went to stay with friends.

Mr. Banerjee did not go to the police. We did not see him for three months. His servant collected the rent.

That year, the Calcutta Municipal Government demolished the shantytown on Sun Yat Sen Street. The police came with batons and heavy boots. They went through the shacks and herded the untouchables onto the street. The police beat and kicked those who resisted. Hired coolies from other shantytowns pulled down the shacks. We shut our windows as dust rose like a gray blanket, blocking out the sunlight. But the closed windows failed to shut out the noise as shacks collapsed, police shouted, men and women pleaded and children cried.

Buddha was not kind to Mr. Lai in 1966. Mr. Lai lost his prostitutes and the shopkeepers' protection money in Chinatown. Two shopkeepers on Sun Yat Sen Street died. Their sons took over the businesses and refused to pay protection money. When Mr. Lai threatened them, they bribed the police to arrest him. Soon all the shopkeepers and vendors in the area paid the police instead of Mr. Lai.

In the same year, Mr. Kumar from Bihar set up a betting operation near Mr. Lai's gambling place in New Market. Mr. Lai tried to shut down the new betting place. Mr. Lai and Mr. Kumar fought. Mr. Kumar stabbed Mr. Lai in the stomach.

The wound festered and Mr. Lai died a month later.

"I always knew that Mr. Lai would come to no good," Mrs. Wong said.

"I knew he would come to a bad end," Mrs. Lim said. "What is going to happen to his wives and children?"

The two Mrs. Lais had no money for their husband's funeral. The Chinese in Chattawalla Gully set up a collection and Mr. Lai was buried. After his father's death, sixteen-year-old Chong, Mr. Lai's eldest son by the Chinese Mrs. Lai, quit school and worked in a tannery. His sister, Mary, went to work in a hairdressing salon. The Chinese Mrs. Lai did laundry.

The Nepalese Mrs. Lai rented the rooftop terrace as a camp ground for Tibetan traders every winter. She also took in laundry. Her oldest son, ten-year-old Sau, washed dishes in a restaurant.

Years later, I heard that five of Mr. Lai's children worked in the Middle East. His daughter Mary married another Chinese who owned a hairdressing salon in Dubai, in the United Arab Emirates. The UAE Government deported her husband for smuggling alcohol into the country. Mary and her family emigrated to San Francisco. The Chinese Mrs. Lai followed her daughter and settled in California.

The Nepalese Mrs. Lai remained in Calcutta. Her three sons worked as cooks in Bahrain and sent money to their mother.

Long Live Mao Tse Tung

When two Communist parties, the Leninist People's United Left Front and the Maoist United Left Front, won the West Bengal general election in 1967, West Bengal became the first province governed by a Communist party in India.

The Communist parties quarrelled between themselves and called frequent general strikes. Businesses moved out of Calcutta. Goods became scarce. Prices soared. Living in Calcutta required patience, the patience to wait in long lines to buy food and clothing, the patience to wait for buses and trams that might not arrive and the patience to wait for protestors and strikers to move on.

In 1968, the central government in New Delhi dissolved the government in West Bengal, declared a province-wide emergency and sent in the army. During the martial-law period, living in Calcutta was like living in the eye of a hurricane. We expected worse to come when the army left.

In 1969, the central government held a provincial election in West Bengal. The two Communist fronts again won a landslide victory. The central government recalled the army.

Chaos returned.

I walked along Bow Bazaar Street. In my shoulder bag, I carried a bottle of water, an umbrella and my mother's visa for residency in Calcutta. I headed for the Indian Immigration Office to renew her visa.

My mother emigrated from China on a Nationalist Chinese passport in the 1920s. When the People's Liberation Army took over China in 1949, Mother became a stateless alien, which required her to renew her visa every year.

I turned into Chattawalla Lane. Behind the high walls of the Dalhousie Girls' School the morning assembly sang:

Showers of blessing, showers of blessings we need....

I stopped, pulled out my handkerchief and wiped my face. The whole city prayed for the monsoon rain, due for over a month. The temperature climbed and the humidity soared. Trees and shrubs yellowed and drooped and the grass in the parks turned to sparse, brown mats. I sighed, opened my umbrella, and walked into the searing sunlight.

When I got to the tram terminal in Dalhousie Square, the trams jammed the tracks. A group of government workers held a rally outside a government building. They spread across the road and blocked all traffic. I decided to walk. As I left the square, I saw a truck parked by the street sign. A worker painted over the sign that read, "Dalhousie Square," changing it to "Behoy Badal Dinesh Bagh." His supervisor sat under a tree, smoking a cigarette.

I called out to the supervisor, "Who or what is Behoy Badal Dinesh Bagh?"

He shrugged, spat and threw his cigarette in the gutter. "I don't know. I am just doing my job."

I shrugged and walked on.

Long Live Mao Tse Tung

The streets were empty of cars and buses, so the pedestrians walked on the road. I joined the crowd walking towards the tram terminal in the Maidan, across from Chowringhee Avenue. Someone carried a portable radio tuned to a station playing songs from Hindi movies. I hummed as I walked. We passed the empty pedestals where the statues of the British Raj used to stand. Slogans plastered the pedestals: "Guns are power," and "Down with Indira Gandhi." The statue of Lenin stood where Lord Curzon used to stand. A cow lay in the shade of one of the pedestals. Its ears flipped from side to side. Its tail brushed the flies off its back as it chewed.

The heat beat down. I took a sip from my water bottle. A man jostled me and another man pushed past me. A woman's sari-end caught on my umbrella. I closed my umbrella and put it inside my shoulder bag.

The Maidan, where once the Gurkhas and the Royal Indian Army drilled under the officers of the British Raj, where once Queen Victoria's viceroys saluted the marching troops under the Union Jack and where once the British officers stood to attention when the bands played "God Save the Queen" or "God Save the King," was reduced now to a vast brown and dusty field, fringed by open air markets, shanty towns, trams and bus terminals.

Shoppers strolled towards the open air market. Women's saris shone brightly against the brown grass. I walked along Chowringhee Avenue, across from the Maidan. Shopkeepers threw water onto the sidewalk outside their shops to keep the dust down. Sweepers swept the garbage and dust onto the street and the passing cars and buses threw the dust and garbage back onto the sidewalk.

I walked to the tram terminal. Passengers milled around the trams. I asked a woman sitting on her bags, "Trams not running?"

"There is a rally or some such nonsense further up the street. The trams and buses could not get through."

I thanked her and kept walking. Further up the Maidan, loudspeakers blared. Pictures of Lenin and Mao danced on top of long bamboo poles. A fire burned at the edge of the Maidan. Pictures of Mrs. Gandhi curled and blackened in the fire. I detoured to avoid the rally and ran into another protest group.

A crowd gathered outside the US Consulate. They chanted "*Mao Tse Tung zindabad* (Long live Mao Tse Tung)" and waved placards that read, "Down with CIA." The Calcuttans blamed the CIA and Mrs. Gandhi for everything from droughts to floods to car accidents. Another supervisor sat under a tree. He smoked and watched as a worker changed the street sign outside the US Consulate from "Harrington Street" to "Ho Chi Min Street." I skirted around the protestors.

When the Chinese government withdrew their Consulate from Calcutta in 1962, the Indian Immigration Department took over the building. The Chinese from all over West Bengal came to this building to renew their visas. The large colonial building with Grecian pillars hid behind a high wall, set back from the street. The houses on this street all had high walls. Trees and bushes screened the buildings, and guards with guns stood at the gates. The former Chinese Consulate House had once belonged to a wealthy British merchant. In the large former dining room, overlooking the garden, the Indians had set up six rusty and dented metal desks. The four ceiling fans stirred the dust and the clerks sat surrounded by mountains of yellowing paper.

A servant came by with a kettle and called out, "*Sahibs, chai*?" The clerks clamoured to be served their tea first.

Long Live Mao Tse Tung

I walked up to the head clerk. He kept his head down over his newspaper. "We are very busy. We cannot attend to your papers today." He put down the newspaper and turned to the man at the desk next to him. They talked about their children's soccer games.

"Can't you add this to the work today?" I asked the back of his head. He ignored me.

I rapped on the desk and raised my voice. "Excuse me," I said and rapped on the desk again.

He turned his head. "What is it? Can't you see I am busy?"

I took a deep breath. "I walked for three hours to get here and I was stopped on the way by the Maoist party. They let me pass because I told them that I have to renew my visa. They wanted to help their Chinese comrade. Should I tell them you are too busy to attend to business? They are rallying outside the US Consulate."

He looked at me for the first time. "Okay. Seeing that you came a long way, I will make an exception and do your papers. I will do it this afternoon."

I nodded. "This afternoon at one, then. Thank you."

I walked towards the back of the former dining room. A row of dented metal folding chairs lined one wall. Eight Chinese spread out on the chairs. Two men dozed, three men talked in low voices, two women bounced their babies on their laps and a woman with short, permed hair sat beside them. They looked up as I approached. I smiled and sat beside the woman. Her name was Silk. She had come from Kalumpang, a hill station in northern West Bengal, to renew her mother's visa.

She was twenty years old, the same age as me, and had worked in a hairdressing salon in Kalumpang since she was thirteen. She wanted to work in her cousin's hairdressing salon in Bombay.

"After I work in my cousin's salon for a few years, I want to open my own salon," she said. "I can make a lot of money in Bombay. The film stars pay their hairdressers well. Most of the actresses have their personal hairdressers. My cousin told me that her friend worked for Mumtaz. You have seen Mumtaz's latest movie?"

I nodded.

"Anyway, the work for the actress is light. She goes on location to all sorts of beautiful places and she works with the famous film stars. I'd love that. What about you?"

I shrugged. "I don't know. I will be sitting for my Cambridge exams next year. After that, I will learn shorthand and typing. With so few jobs around, I probably need a BA to be a secretary. Most of my friends are getting married."

Silk shuddered. "Not for me. For the next few years, anyway. Mother wants me to get married. That's why I want to go to Bombay."

I grinned. "I know what you mean. Five kids in as many years, work from six in the morning to twelve at night. But seriously, my choices are limited. If I am very, very lucky, I can get a job, which will probably pay very little."

Silk said, "Like me?"

I laughed. "No. Secretaries don't get tips. Chances are I will stay at home, look after my brother's five kids and get kicked out when the kids grow up, say in five years' time."

"There is another option, you know." Silk said, "You could marry a Chinese who emigrated to the West, like Canada or Australia. They usually want girls who can speak English."

I nodded. "I had a few friends who did that. I would like to go to a western country. It is scary, though, to go to a totally different place that you have only read about. But, I won't worry about it yet. Calcutta is a crazy city. It takes up so much of your time just to get things done. You know we had food rationing until about two or three years ago?"

"Yeah. We had it in Kalumpang as well, but there was plenty of food if you had the money."

"The rationing in Calcutta was serious. We had to line up for hours to get rice and wheat early in the morning. The merchants added sand and grit to the grain when the supply ran low in the evenings."

Silk shook her head, "It was not as bad in Kalumpang."

"The bread line was the worst. I used to get up at five in the morning and line up for two hours to buy a loaf of bread. Once I stood outside the bakery on Chowringhee Avenue. You know the one near the Grand Hotel?"

Silk nodded.

"Well, a group of foreign tourists strolled by. They stayed and took pictures of the lineups."

"Did you smile for the camera?"

"Hah. I was wearing a cardigan with a hole on my left shoulder. I had my hand over the hole. The tourists probably thought I was posing for them." We laughed.

We got our papers at four o'clock. Silk and I got on a tram. She got off at the Park Street stop. I wished her luck in getting to Bombay. Silk ran from the tram stop to the sidewalk. At the curb, she turned, waved and plunged into the crowd.

As the tram clanged towards the Maidan, the crowd grew thicker. A protest group blocked the tram tracks. All the passengers got off the tram and walked. The protestors parted for a truck full of young men with red berets. The young men on the truck shouted slogans and waved placards with pictures of Lenin.

As I neared home, I ran into two noisy groups at the intersection of Bentinck and Bow Bazaar Streets. One group wore red sashes and waved red banners that read "Workers' Party (Marxist)." The other group wore red berets and waved red banners and placards that read "Workers' Union."

The two groups crashed into each other in a tangle of banners, signs, waving fists and kicking limbs. Two red sashes grabbed a red beret and kicked him to the ground. A shouting group rushed to the shops. They forced open shop doors and ran inside, pushing, shouting and fighting with each other. A red beret tore into the storage boxes of a toy shop and threw dolls and tiny tea sets at a red sash. A red sash grabbed a toy car and put it in his pocket. Next door, ten men fought to get at the boxes of candies in a broken, glass display case.

Another group of red berets surrounded a parked car. Broken glass flew as they smashed in the windows. A red sash threw a piece of burning wood into the car.

I turned into Sun Yat Sen Street and ran. A crowd ran with me. A woman, with a child in her arms and another hanging on to her sari, tripped and fell. The children screamed. The woman crawled into a doorway and covered the children with her body. I tripped over a shoe stuck to the hot asphalt of the road. A little girl sat on the curb and cried. She had dropped her red ball. The ball rolled into the middle of the road and the running crowd kicked her ball away. A woman pushed her way through the crowd to the child, picked her up and hurried into a doorway.

The shouts and screams grew faint. I stopped, took a deep breath and gagged. I stood before the Sun Yat Sen Street garbage dump.

Long Live Mao Tse Tung

On the sidewalk, the Calcutta Municipal Corporation had built a low brick-enclosure the size of a garbage truck, with three walls and no roof. The people living in the area threw their garbage into the enclosure. Once a week, the government sent a garbage truck and cleared the enclosure.

Three weeks before, the garbage pickup crew had gone on strike. Garbage filled the enclosure and spilled onto the street and the sidewalk. Dogs, crows and flies rummaged through the grey and rotting piles. Two cows nosed at a pile of yellowing lettuce in the middle of the road. Rag-pickers had built two shacks against the outside walls of the garbage enclosure. Garbage engulfed the shacks.

A woman came out of a shack with a torn wicker basket balanced on her head. Across from me, a sweeper tilted his wheelbarrow and spilled more garbage over a pile already flattened by passing vehicles. The woman walked towards the new pile. A dog and an urchin followed.

Taking shallow breaths, I hugged the wall across from the dump and picked my way through the slime spread across the sidewalk. My left hip bumped into a potted ivy. The ivy hung from a hook on the wall, the broken pot held together by string. Someone had rescued the plant from the garbage and tried to keep it alive. I touched the tiny dark green leaves and looked around.

Stucco flaked from the grey buildings around the garbage dump. Washing, hung out to dry, hid the broken railings of balconies where people cooked, ate and slept. A woman threw pieces of meat, carrot and potato peelings from one balcony. Two dogs, two urchins and a woman pounced on the morsels.

I looked down at the green plant, took out my water bottle and emptied the water over the ivy.

Made in the USA
Charleston, SC
27 June 2016